Though she grew up in Macon, Georgia, and later attended Wesleyan College, Cheri Dennis has lived in Atlanta since 1980. Her major was art, and she worked as a graphic artist in Augusta, Atlanta, and Baltimore as she followed her husband during his medical training. When their first daughter was born in 1976, she became a full-time mom to what would later be three girls. Since an early age, she always dreamed of writing. As she grew older, learning more about her family's history became a passion. This book was an opportunity to combine the two interests.

Dedicated to my three daughters: Mary Clare, Catherine, and Caroline. Look deep and tell the truth.

Cheri Dennis

DEAR MR. ELLAMAE

AUSTIN MACAULEY PUBLISHERS™

LONDON • CAMBRIDGE • NEW YORK • SHARJAH

Ordering Information
Quantity sales: Special discounts are available on quantity purchases by corporations, associations, and others. For details, contact the publisher at the address below.

Publisher's Cataloging-in-Publication data
Dennis, Cheri
Dear Mr. Ellamae

ISBN 9781649795564 (Paperback)
ISBN 9781649795571 (ePub e-book)

Library of Congress Control Number: 2021916685

www.austinmacauley.com/us

First Published 2021
Austin Macauley Publishers LLC
40 Wall Street, 33rd Floor, Suite 3302
New York, NY 10005
USA

mail-usa@austinmacauley.com
+1 (646) 5125767

Timeline

August 17, 1871

Joseph Oliver Ellis is born (father).

March 1874

Susan Dilworth Choate Ellis is born (mother).

June 5, 1890

George Forrest League is born.

December 1, 1893

Joseph O. Ellis – Susan Dilworth Choate marry.

November 2, 1894

Joseph Edward Ellis is born.

August 1897

Charles W. Ellis is born.

July 9, 1899

Ellamae Ellis is born.

August 23, 1902

Eugene Dupree Ellis is born.

1905

Nell Choate is born.

August 6, 1906

Dilworth Choate Ellis is born.

1914-18

World War I.

1916

Ellamae graduates Lanier High School.

1916 – 17

Ellamae attends Wesleyan College for Women.

April 6, 1917

The United States enters the war under President Woodrow Wilson.

June 4, 1917

Joseph Edward Ellis enlists at age 23.

June 27, 1917

Ellamae marries George Forrest League.

November 11, 1918

WWI Ends.

1919

KLM Royal Dutch Airlines begins operation.

March 20, 1919

Jean League is born.

March 1920

Marjorie Ellis is born.

March 27, 1921

Joseph Choate League is born.

1922

Ellamae & George Forrest League divorce.

1922

Ellamae moves to Katherine Courts Apts.
Ellamae begins work for Dunwody & Oliphant Architects.
Ellamae begins correspondence courses at New York's Beaux-Arts Institute of Design.

1926

First flights from Candler Field, now Hartsfield-Jackson Atlanta International Airport.

1927

Ellamae to study in France with Nell Choate.

September 1928

Ellamae returns from France on the SS France.
Ellamae joins the firm of Oliphant & Shelverton Architects

1929

Pan American World Airways begins service.
Ellamae and children move to College Street.

October 24, 1929

"Black Thursday" Market Crash.

1929–39

The Great Depression.

April 1933

Bill Oliphant dies.
Ellamae passes boards.

1934

Ellamae begins her own practice at 607 Grand Bldg.

1937

Jean graduates from A.L. Miller High School.
Jean attends Choate School in Brookline,
Massachusetts.

1939

Jean attends Radcliffe College.
Pan American begins trans-Atlantic flights.
Joe to Georgia Institute of Technology.

1940

Ellamae builds her home at 1790 Waverland Drive.

1941 – 1945

World War II.

September 29, 1943

Joe marries Mary Jane Proebstle in Waco, TX.

Jean graduates from the Harvard School of Design.

1944

Ellamae is admitted to the American Institute of Architects.

July 17, 1944

Joseph Choate League Jr. is born.

1945

Firm name changed to LEAGUE, WARREN & RILEY.

October 5, 1945

Cheryl Jean League is born.

1945 – 46

Joe Sr. separates from Army Air Corps active duty and moves the family to Macon.

February 27, 1950

George Forrest League dies.

June 25, 1950 – 53

Korean War.

1952

First commercial jet service begins.

1953

Ellamae begins Macon Hospital Project.

January 1, 1954

Joseph Oliver Ellis dies.

October 8, 1954

Jean League marries Charles Edward Newton III.

1955

Susan Dilworth Choate Ellis dies.

December 17, 1956

Suzy Newton is born.

1963

Ellamae establishes the Macon chapter of the AIA and serves as the first president; she also serves as vice-president of Georgia's state chapter of the AIA.

April 30, 1960

Edith Newton is born.

October 16, 1962

Cuban Missile Crisis.

August 14, 1962

Meredith Ann League is born.

1963

Ellamae becomes the first president of the Georgia Council of Architects, now the Georgia Association of Architects.

March 6, 1963

Joseph Edward Ellis dies

November 22, 1963

President John F. Kennedy is assassinated.

September 1964

Public schools in Macon begin integrating.

1968

Ellamae becomes the first woman in the state of Georgia to be invested as a Fellow the American Institute of Architects.

Phase I of the Grand Opera House renovation begins.

1969

Ellamae receives the Wesleyan College Alumni Award for Distinguished Achievement.

July 20, 1969

Neil Armstrong and Buzz Aldrin land the Apollo II lunar module "Eagle" on the moon.

1970

Ellamae receives the Ivan Allen Sr. Award for community service for the North Georgia Chapter of the AIA.

1973

Watergate Scandal.

August. 9, 1974

President Richard Milhouse Nixon resigns.

April 30, 1975

Vietnam War ends after fall of Saigon.

October 1975

Ellamae closes her office.

February 1, 1981

Eugene Dupree Ellis dies.

March 30, 1981

Attempted assassination of President Ronald Reagan.

1982

Ellamae becomes the first architectural recipient of Bernard B. Rothschild Award.

March 19, 1989

Dilworth Choate Ellis dies.

March 4, 1991

Ellamae Ellis League dies.

Foreword

"I am almost a hundred years old; waiting for the end, and thinking about the beginning.

There are things I need to tell you, but would you listen if I told you how quickly time passes?

I know you are unable to imagine this.

Nevertheless, I can tell you that you will awake someday to find that your life has rushed by at a speed at once impossible and cruel. The most intense moments will seem to have occurred only yesterday and nothing will have erased the pain and pleasure, the impossible intensity of love and its dog-leaping happiness, the bleak blackness of passions unrequited, unexpressed or unresolved.

You get old and you realize there are no answers, just stories…"

MEG ROSOFF/GARRISON KEILLOR[1]

I was inspired to write the story of my grandmother long before I read this quote because of who she was and because

---

[1] Art Magazine Post, March 9, 2014.

she influenced so many. Her influence was her work and style and the beautiful homes and buildings she designed, but very few people could see past her façade to see her heart. Like the quote says, she grew quite old and had so many stories and if she could tell us now about some of the most important ones, I am betting that we might all be surprised.

My story is mostly true. I have made every effort to bring you a factual account but admit that I have filled in some gaps to keep you engaged.

When I did take this license, I tried to embellish with the heart and mind of the people as I knew them and mix in just a little common sense.

The journey through the piles of photos, letters, and interviews often made me cry, not with sadness as much as with awe and longing to have treasured more of these people's stories while they were living and at my fingertips. My biggest regret is the gaps that I never asked about when their minds were crisp and the feelings so available.

I pray that I haven't tarnished memories or slighted any influences, but I have risked all this to tell the truest and most loving account of these important people who left their mark on so many. I loved them dearly despite their flaws and humanness, and it is my desire that you will admire their gifts rather than get bogged down in their "not so pretty" qualities.

The story that I am telling here is not about designing buildings or being the first or greatest, but it is about relationships and events and births and deaths and all the parts that go into life, and how all the parts fit together to build people.

I am certain that we don't know what makes us who we are while we are busy living. For instance, I am certain that my father never understood the impact that his mother's circumstances had on his life until he was older. People and events mold us in ways that are sometimes profound, and we realize it at the time. Other things mold us more subtly and we realize over time that those impressions stay with us in ways we never imagined they would. Siblings may have been present at the same event and one might come away with one memory and the other come away with an entirely different impression. As we grow and live, we realize that we weren't hiding something about ourselves, but that we had not understood our ability to block out what brings us to our truth.

Twice in my life I have had a close family member die and their son or daughter put them to rest with a diminished love for them because of what they didn't know about them. Secrets sometimes are kept because we think we are protecting someone or because we are embarrassed or ashamed, but are often the very ingredients that bring us to a deeper empathy and understanding and opens the floodgates of real love. This little story is intended to do just that. I hope it inspires others to dig a little and by default, love more through understanding.

This is a book that each and every one of us wants to write about our family and how uniquely we all fit together and become a story. Mine includes an accomplished, pioneering grandmother, which makes it worth telling to a larger audience than just my immediate family. You be the judge of my ability to tell it in a way that makes it a tale worth reading.

Chapter 1

"I think everything in life is art. What you do.
How you dress. The way you love someone,
and how you talk. Your smile and your
personality. What you believe in, *and* all your
dreams. The way you drink your tea. How
you decorate your home. Or party. Your
grocery list. The food you make. How your
writing looks. And the way you feel. Life is
art."

HELENA BONHAM CARTER[2]

March 2, 1991

Ellamae

I know every board, every nail in every room because I
chose every one and picked the spots for each window and
door. I have listened for fifty-one of my ninety-one years to
their sounds as they have kept me company. We are so
intimate, this house and me.

---

[2] Wild Woman Sisterhood, Blog by Tara Isis.

"Mrs. League, Mrs. League, can you hear me? Squeeze my hand, dear. Nothing, Mr. Joe."

Oh, I hear you, Naomi. I do, but all my words are gone. I'm in here alright, but I am alone in my head.

It's not bad, you know. Like a watching a play. Actually, I like it here, though I am ready to die.

I have been at this dying business for a good while now. Never dreamed it would be this way or take so long. Not the way I planned it at all.

"Nothing to eat for nine days now…just a little water on her lips is all."

"Thanks, Naomi. Jean will be by in an hour, and Mary Jane will drop by on her way home for lunch. I let Meals on Wheels know to stop all deliveries. Call me if there are any changes."

"Sure, Mr. Joe. Won't be long. Things are shuttin' down and I can hear the rattles."

Joe is in the hall and the floor boards are very quiet there. The very moment his feet hit the stairs, those boards will whine. They groan even louder when his feet hit the landing. Did he forget something? No, he's moving again, headed to the door. The door isn't sticking, so it must be sunny. Once he is out of the garage, I can hear his muffled crunch on the pine straw and figure just how far down the driveway he parked.

I'm cold, but that doesn't mean anything anymore, since Joe put air-conditioning in my house. I was perfectly content with my attic fan and night breezes and the windows wide. It's like a divorce from the weather, having the very air I breathe so controlled and always the same. The smells, when my windows were open, told me what season it was.

I can't know the weather unless it's raining, and I can still hear that on the roof.

Damn! A switch…a hiss. That's another thing I never wanted in my house, a television. I wish Marsha were here. Younger than me but long dead… I really miss her. She really knew me well, and so like me she was. Never would have turned a TV on while I am dying. She knew the value of *quiet*.

"Come on down. The price is right," the television squeals.

That awful, twangy music and loud people. I want my quiet back. I know she's bored, sitting in a chair, this Naomi person, waiting for me to die but hoping that I don't because each day fattens her check. Not her fault, really. Just doing her job. Clearly, I am still alive or she wouldn't be here. No need to sit with the dead.

Chapter 2

"There are only two days in the year
that nothing can be done. One is called
yesterday and the other is called *tomorrow*,
so *today* is the right day to love, believe, do
and mostly live."

DALAI LAMA[3]

1946

The rain is pounding on the shingles of the roof but thank God it is not colder, turning it to sleet. Despite the gloominess of the day, Ellamae is over-the-top with excitement because Joe is home to Macon with his little family in tow. Bill Drinnon, Macon's newspaper photographer, is en route, and Mother, brother Joe Jr., and I are expected any minute for the camera to document that Joe and his family have set up their life on Shaw Drive. Daddy had been here for a few months making ready for Mother to move and bring his family finally home. Mother

[3] https://wisdomquotes.com/dalia-lama-quotes-tenzin-gyatso/

had been in Margate City, New Jersey with her parents, sister, and brothers since my birth, all the time getting accustomed to wrangling two young children. I was born there so Mother would have help with young Sparky (a nickname given my brother by Daddy's copilot) while Daddy transitioned from military life following the end of his duty.

Joe was twenty months and I only four months, before Ellamae or Jean ever laid eyes on us. We had swapped our New Jersey grandparents for two new doting relatives and were certainly not lacking in love and attention. Aunt Jean, whom I was named after, was a freshly practicing architect. The war was over, thank the Lord, and Ellamae's career was taking off. Just the previous year, she had been admitted to the American Institute of Architects, and although the letter arrived addressed to "Mr." Ellamae League, it did not tarnish her pride. She was growing ever more accustomed to assumptions that she was a he because even in 1945, women were few in the profession of architecture. In a small town like Macon, especially following the war, women had stepped up to replace the men in many jobs, but architecture remained almost exclusively a man's role. Contractors were still men as were bricklayers, electricians, plasterers and so forth. A slim, blonde woman on a job site was not a common occurrence, and even more unusual was one who was in charge and giving directions. It is safe to guess that many struggled with the role reversal.

Visible in everyone was relief from the suffering that came after the horrors of the atomic bomb. War-ravaged soldiers, husbands, and sons were returning from the war.

Clearly, things were looking up in everyone's world and most especially in Ellamae's world.

She must have been experiencing feelings that she'd not had since her high school days at Lanier, surrounded by her four adoring brothers and with no sense of her life falling off the tracks in the way that it ultimately did after she met and married George Forrest League. Ellamae was not one to slip into self-pity or to dwell on her failings. After all, hadn't she put all that so far away in her memory bank and didn't it seem so distant from her world now?

It is hard to guess when the actual moment occurred that Ellamae made the decision to wipe her ex-husband from her life and that of her children and a city, but I believe it was a conscious decision. Maybe her parents advised her to move forward in a positive way, or maybe divorce was so unusual in 1921, that it was her youthful wisdom that nudged her to go forward with no animosity or explanation for walking away from the father of her two children.

The newspaper picture of us had no sooner hit the doorsteps than George Forrest League, from his kitchen in Warner Robins, not twenty or so miles south of Macon, felt his stomach flop. There in front of him was the announcement that his estranged son had returned to Macon following the war. I cannot guess what ran through his head because I know so little about him, but after twenty-two years of absence, he picked up the phone.

Daddy, having arrived at Ellamae's house just minutes before the phone rang, ran to the landing where the one house phone was located and breathlessly answered the ring.

******

Ellamae, until the day she died, never locked her doors. Her redwood, split- level home had many exterior doors, which was a recurring feature of the homes she designed, including the one I would later move to when I was five. Ours was built just a little farther up the street on Waverland Drive, where it still sits today. Growing up there in the close proximity of our grandmother had many advantages for Joe Jr. and me, and one was that we always had free rein of her house.

Marsha, Ellamae's maid was delivered to work each morning by her close friend's husband, Benny Stokes. Benny had a car and at that time, and he worked for the railroad. Later he would distinguish himself as Macon's first black bus driver with The Bibb County Transit Company. Bennie's wife, Birdie Mae Stokes was a precious, childless woman who loved other people's children to fill the void, but the truth is she just loved everybody. Black or white—it made no difference. She would babysit for us often, and her permissive indulgence kept her at the forefront of our list of favorites.

Marsha commanded and was given as much respect from us as my grandmother. She had her very own bathroom where she kept her things and washed up, and my brother and I knew that under no circumstances, regardless of whether Marsha was there or not, should we ever darken that door. It may have been locked, though I doubt it, but I swear to you, I never set one foot inside. Only one other bathroom existed in the house, and if it happened to be occupied, well, you just had to wiggle and wait! If my grandmother built it because she didn't want Marsha to use her bathroom, I couldn't say. Maybe a bathroom for "help" was common, but that aspect was never suggested to my brother and me. It was described to us as Marsha's private domain.

At noon every day, Ellamae drove her Buick the five or six miles home from her office and Marsha served her lunch. I mean served in the truest sense because Ellamae was very formal about meals. She would sit alone in her dining room, with her brass call bell, and Marsha served her the main meal of the day after which she went up to her bedroom, took her dress and shoes off, and in her slip or robe, she would throw herself on her bed and read through the newspaper until she fell asleep. After a short nap, refreshed, she would powder her face, redress and tidy her bed, and head downstairs, where Marsha would be waiting. The two of them would then get in her Buick, Marsha always on the back passenger side, and the two would merrily chat while Ellamae drove her home. Ellamae would drive back to her office and work late into the afternoon, and this was her daily routine with the only exceptions being Saturday and Sunday. This particular day was like all others except that Daddy had appeared there that afternoon for who knows what reason, just as the phone started to ring.

"Hello."

"Hello. This is Forrest League speaking. Please don't hang up."

Since his father had never been in his life, Daddy was stunned to realize that he was speaking to his father, a total and complete stranger. In some of Daddy's writings he said:

"I was never curious about him (unlike all the movie stories) and I knew very little about him. I think his home was Rome, Georgia. I think he was in the military service, probably a private in the infantry, since there was a military camp here then, Camp Wheeler. I never heard from him, or even about him, anytime, until then. He called my mother's home and by chance, I answered the phone. He was in Warner Robins, a town near here that had grown up around Robins Air Force Base. He was working at the base. He asked if I would meet with him, even for a short time. I agreed to do that. I went to the address that he gave me. It turned out to be a cheap apartment in a housing project. He made a bad appearance, age about middle forties, bald, a couple of inches shorter than I was, and not too clean. He introduced me to two sons, maybe 10 and 14. He had remarried but I didn't see a wife. The boys never opened their mouths. He said nothing that was meaningful or interesting and I stayed less than fifteen minutes. I wished I hadn't seen him. My imagination was better than real life. You see, I never missed having a father, because I never had one. I heard from a co-worker of his that he died at 50."

Daddy also wrote:

Within a few months of my birth Mother and George Forrest League were separated with much bitterness, and later divorced. I have absolutely no memory of my father and he was never discussed by my mother or by my grandparents. Not a word. There was never a call or a letter. I learned later that my grandfather threw him out and obtained a court order that stipulated that he could never visit this city or see us or my mother. (letter from Joseph C. League to Mr. William League, Aug.14, 2002)

Daddy never spoke of his meeting with his father to anyone but my mother. He certainly had no reason to put a ripple on his mother's smooth sea or his sister's rosy world. Knowing Daddy as I did, and being so close to him in the months after Mother died, I learned that he bore huge pain that he never shared. There were many scars of not having had a father in his life, and Ellamae was a shining example of stoicism who taught him by her example to suck it up. I doubt that she ever complained of her poor marriage or made any reference to missing having a husband to share the load. To her, George Forrest simply was no longer a factor in any respect except her last name.

Mother later recalled that Daddy had been disappointed when he met his father, and he warned him never to contact his mother or sister, making it clear that he never wanted to see him again. Mother also said that from that day forward, Daddy would brush his hair vigorously each day for fear that he might become as bald as his father, whom he described to her as "bald as a billiard ball."

I can imagine that Daddy was so disappointed. His mother, though certainly not conventional, was successful and strong and never felt the need to diminish any vision that Daddy and Jean might have conjured of a father.

It's hard to imagine that my father and aunt repeatedly said that since they never had a dad, they never missed him.

I can grasp the concept only because my siblings and cousins, like me, never remembered any mention of him or suggestion that he ever existed. I can honestly say that I was close to eighteen years old before it ever occurred to me to ask about him or even wonder what his name was. I was simply as though he never was! Growing up in Macon, everyone knew my grandmother and my dad, but never did anyone inquire about a grandfather, know him, or have a story about him. The one picture I have of him I found after Daddy died, and I got it from Daddy's half-brother, George.

Joe and I were surely the most fortunate of Ellamae's grandchildren, who would later number five, because we were the first. Actually, the first on both sides. Daddy's sister, Jean, was fresh out of Harvard and plowing on to the architectural scene. She was a slim and pretty, brown-haired girl, in a postwar world with many suitors like her very pretty mother. Ellamae built her house after Daddy was at Georgia Tech, so she knew he'd likely never live in it. The two-bedroom house, by 1940 standards had a very large bedroom on the second floor that was designed for two people. The entry to the room was flanked on both sides by built-in drawers and mirrors as well as two closets. The room contained two full-size beds and a long, floor-to-ceiling window on one side that allowed you a view of the front door. Jean graduated from the Harvard School of Design in 1944 and returned to Macon and shared the home with her mother. The house's only bathroom, except, of course, Marsha's room, was on the level with this bedroom. A narrow staircase rose steeply to a third floor that was the guest room, or maybe it was called a sleeping loft. On the outside wall, a door led to a deck that had a narrow, covered area and the rest was open. Another steep ladder of stairs led down to a terraced, grassy area that ran the length of the living room. The side that looked toward the backyard overlooked a huge magnolia tree that was hefty enough to climb. In the bedroom were twin beds that were pushed together, and they were the largest, fluffiest, deepest mattresses that I can ever remember seeing. How I loved to sleep there. When I spent the night there by myself, without Joe, I got to sleep in Ellamae's room. I really felt grown up when that happened.

The upper deck had a storage room under the overhang of the roof and the door to it was never locked. Some furniture pieces were stored there and lots of books and letters were boxed in the recesses. Before my grandmother died, I spent many hours there snooping in her treasures, sometimes with her knowledge and sometimes, well, you finish the sentence. My brother, sister and the cousins likely ended up with the furniture, and my father and Aunt Jean likely went through the rest, but I am so grateful for that early look into her life. Some of my finds inspired me to keep digging. My most vivid memory was of some field orders and maps from World War I that I found. They belonged to Bill Oliphant, and it appeared that he was a courier on the front lines in France. They were in a well-seasoned and worn leather pouch that probably went around his waist strapped under his clothing. The maps and orders that it held were shaped by the bend of the leather and were crispy and yellow with age. They were signed by field generals, and at the time they seemed important to me. I knew they would tell me a story someday when I was older.

The smell of leather was loud, and I wondered who the carrier had been to Ellamae.

On the particular day of the photo of Joe's family, likely my grandmother had no idea the event that the newspaper article would trigger, and I am almost certain that she never knew.

That may sound strange today in our "tell all" culture of truth, but then, these sorts of omissions were viewed quite differently. At least in Ellamae's family, unpleasant or unnecessary information was just allowed to fade away if it was considered irrelevant. It is not for me to judge, but there are benefits to both ways of looking at it. Had Ellamae been trained to dig deeper or search a past, she might never have married George Forrest, which means I would not be telling you this story.

Chapter 3

"I've never met a strong person with an easy past. Be proud of your scars and take pride that you are still standing."

–UNKNOWN

1899

The pacing began on July 9, 1899, as Joseph Oliver Ellis wore a path in the boards of the home he rented with his family on Magnolia Street. The house, right next to the pump station, would soon be a tighter fit because his first daughter arrived before the day was over. Two boys (Edward, five, and Charles, two) already kept him and Susie in a whirl, so Joe was truly hoping for a girl.

There was other excitement in Macon that year, and the Ellis household was all abuzz with the news that the first horseless carriage was coming to town. A carnival and floral parade would debut the automobile, and it was rumored that a local doctor had his eye on buying it.[4]

---

[4] *The Macon Telegraph*, Saturday morning, October 14, 1899:2.

"I can't imagine it being of much use to us," Joe remarked to his wife later that evening as she tended their infant daughter. "Our roads and alleys are much better suited to horses. Our money will be better spent on a bigger house because we will soon be busting at the seams when this little beauty gets on her feet." It would be many years before cars were plentiful in Macon, but in just a few short months, a new house would be found and the family would move.

******

By all accounts, Ellamae gave Susie and Joe much joy. She was smart and pretty and eventually flanked by four brothers who adored her. When Ellamae was three, brother Eugene was born, and three years later, her fourth brother, Dilworth, joined the clan. It would be 1920, almost fourteen years, until another daughter would arrive in the Ellis family. Before Ellamae's younger brothers came, the family had moved to 433 Carling Avenue and then to 115 Rembert Avenue in Macon. From there, they would move to Miami in 1922, but Ellamae would stay behind.

I know very little about the events of Ellamae's childhood other than that she attended Lanier High School and graduated in 1916. Her prom cards were full, and it appeared that she had a life much like you'd expect of a young lady in 1916 and 1917. The following year, she attended Wesleyan Conservatory on College Street, just up the hill from her first home. In April 1917, the United States entered World War I under President Woodrow Wilson.

Just a few months later, on June 27, 1917, Ellamae married George Forrest League.

******

"Joe, come right away. Did you bring the paper?" Susie Ellis was out of breath as she pushed little Ellamae's pram onto the porch. It was not very cold for a December afternoon so close to Christmas.

"Everyone is saying the Wright Brothers have flown an aeroplane! I want to read it for myself. Those boys have certainly made a place for themselves in the history books by keeping that machine in the air. Bring the boys in and we can read all about it."

Slowly, aviation moved from airships and the Zeppelin to gliders and now a modified glider that could be controlled and powered by a machine.

Sadly, just passed-on accounts would have to do for a good while because news traveled slowly, and only a few newspapers in the States even mentioned the Wright Brothers' flight in 1903. It would be June of 1907 before the United States would develop major public interest in flying, and that was sparked by a building dedicated to aviation at the Jamestown Exposition. Airplanes would begin to take on great importance at this time, as they advanced and played a significant role in World War I. After the war, the airplane developed commercial application, and soon passenger planes would emerge on the scene.[5]

Joe Ellis was wide-eyed and full of excitement at the news. Perhaps one day, he would be able to climb into a machine that could fly. *What a wonderful time to be alive!* he thought. Cars replacing horses right before their eyes, and Macon building new buildings all the time!

******

Here it is, June 27, 1917, and Joe Ellis was pacing again but not filled with hope and joy. This time was very different. This time, his only daughter was getting married and he was filled with dread. He wondered how they had come to this day. Ellamae had always been strong-minded for a girl, but he credited her brothers with that, though in so many ways, she was the toughest of the lot. With four boys around who found her suitor lacking and a father who had his doubts, why was she going through with this?

A letter from J. O. Smith came in April to Ellamae upon learning of her up-coming marriage. He spoke of his fear of going off to war and likely never coming home but said he lacked the desire to come home, knowing he would never have a chance with her. He wrote he would likely never see her again but that George Forrest was a very lucky man.

---

5 Elizabeth Howell, "The Wright Brothers and the First Airplane Flight," www.space.com.

Yet another young man, named Bogart, begged Ellamae for a picture of herself to take off to war with him, and he directly questioned her in his letter.

"Do you care for, like, or love this man from Louisiana?" His letter was dated January 5, 1917, a good six months before her marriage, so obviously, her plan to marry was not made hastily.

Daddy mentioned in some of his writings that more than once, one of Ellamae's beaux asked him for his blessings to propose to his mother, but she never accepted. According to him, she never came close. Life on her own terms seemed to suit her, though she enjoyed dating, parties, and entertaining. Knowing this convinced me that she hadn't married George Forrest because she was seeking a husband, so something else prompted her.

Notice that I always refer to her husband by both of his names and that is because I am not sure what she called him or the name he preferred to be called. I have a small Bible that he gave her with an inscription that reads:

To: Ellamae, Easter 1917
From: Forrest

I would have then assumed Forrest was preferred, but I never saw it written that way again.

Woodrow Wilson was avoiding dragging the US into the war to end all wars but at the same time building forces and training men. Camp Wheeler, just outside of Macon, was designed for just that purpose and was bursting at the seams with young men, many of whom were seeking love and attachments.

Ellamae's own oldest brother, Edward, wrote to his aunt that he knew he would not get to finish college because he and his fraternity brothers at Mercer University would need to enlist. And enlist he did, just twenty-three days before his sister's nuptials.

It must be the war. It had to be the war, Joe Ellis thought to himself. It had everyone doing strange things and acting impulsively. World War I shocked the world because of the huge number of casualties and the atrocities that were being reported. Young American men were training to join the fight as the war raged on in Europe. Many were at Camp Wheeler and with the prospects of the United States entering the war growing more certain, many were in search of love and a reason to return.

******

April 16, 1912

Ellamae and her friends met in the hallway before class, and everybody was speaking in hushed tones and crying and reading from the papers.

At breakfast, Joe Ellis delivered the solemn news of the Titanic slipping into the icy sea and, fearing the worst, they were not holding out much hope for survivors. The family ate in near silence while each one digested the news and all the pictures they could conjure in their minds. An inky sea full of ice had swallowed up some of America's finest and wealthiest people. Weren't there lifeboats? How could it sink? It was unsinkable, right? Why couldn't they be rescued?

Ellamae's friend Gertrude could not be consoled, and she held tight to her friend, hoping she could slip through the crowd unnoticed. Ellamae pulled her along until they got to a higher floor, and then she saw Sara waving at her and screaming above the mayhem, "Wait, you two!"

"Mama was so upset. She said I didn't even have to come to school. I wanted to, though. I just had to keep moving. What could have possibly gone wrong? An iceberg couldn't sink a huge ship, could it?" asked Ellamae.

"No. No, Ellamae. Absolutely not. My pop said they built that ship so it couldn't sink. Finest ship ever built," said Sara.

A sobbing Gertrude decried that she would never feel safe on a vast, wide ocean on any kind of ship. "How can we ever believe that a ship cannot sink if the Titanic can?"

As the days wore on, the news continued to shock the world about that fateful night on a ship ill-prepared for its doom. In just two years, the papers and newsreels would be full of stories about the assassination of Archduke Franz Ferdinand of Austria and his wife. As they rode in a town car, a Serbian ran up and shot them at point-blank range. Young men and women in America had to grapple with concepts like nationalism and the alliances being formed in a far-away place that was steaming with anger and building towards war. Germany, Austria-Hungary, and Italy stood against Russia, France, and Britain, though by 1914, Italy had changed sides. Germany and Britain were competing for naval superiority. Other countries were building military forces to compete on the world stage. It all erupted when the assassination occurred and the powers took sides and World War I began. On April 6, 1917, the US entered the war following the sinking of the passenger ship – the British ocean liner *RMS Lusitania* and other hostilities. A telegram intercepted by the Brits suggested that Germany would form an alliance with Mexico, our neighbor, and they would attack us.

In an incredibly short time, the US amassed a full-scale fighting force with the help of conscription. The involvement of women put pressure on Woodrow Wilson to allow women to vote. America's efforts in the war helped lead the allied powers to victory within six months. Following the war, the US was elevated as a military and economic power in the world, and women began assuming new positions and attention.

******

What I have been able to discover about George Forrest prior to his wedding day is that he completed a draft board registration card on June 1, 1917, just four days before his twenty-seventh birthday and twenty-six days from his wedding. His birthplace is listed as Haralson County, Georgia, and his occupation as an adding machine mechanic employed by Burroughs Adding Machine Company in Shreveport, Louisiana. George Forrest claimed to have served two months in the military as a private in the infantry in Georgia. He claimed exemption from the draft on the grounds of 'physical disability.' He listed his address 115 Rembert Avenue in Macon, which is very curious because he stated he was 'single' and yet this was the address of Ellamae's parents. In the next section of the form, George Forrest described himself as five feet, eleven inches tall, slender, with light blue eyes, and dark brown hair, and he filled in a space that asked if he was bald with 'no.' The form was filled out in his own handwriting.[6]

******

The day a father should be joyful about was here, and though every bone in his body felt dread, Joe worked to keep his spirits up for his darling wife. Susie took to her bed the night before and barely kept her chin up for the ceremony. It was going to be a long, hard day, and the Ellises would face it with as much hope as they could muster, denying all the flares that were bursting in their heads.

George Forrest League arrived as though from dust. In addition to being quite average-looking and lacking the fine attributes of many of Ellamae's other suitors, he was also nine years older than her. Maybe that was it. Maybe he just appealed to some deep longing for the adventure that lay beneath her surface. Perhaps his age made him seem more mature and modern. Even she did not profess great love. The draft registration I found suggests that perhaps George Forrest was drafted and that this was what brought him to Macon. At that time, President Wilson was keeping the United States neutral, but after the Zimmerman Telegram exposed Germany's efforts to escalate pressure on Mexico to attack the US, it was clear that we would enter the Great War. The Selective Service Act was passed just six weeks

---

[6] U.S. World War I Draft Registration Cards, 1917-1918, Provo, UT, USA: www.ancestry.com, 2005.

after the United States entered World War I on May 18, 1917. This gave President Wilson the ability to draft all young men between the ages of twenty-one and thirty to register for military service.

Camp Wheeler added even more young recruits as the United States entered the war. In April, it happened. Now barely two months into it and Ellamae stood at the altar with a man she hardly knew, hardly loved, and was staking her life on. He had a sketchy story of a family, some sisters in Rome, Georgia, some relatives in New York, and some in Shreveport perhaps, but none she knew or had ever met. Certainly, the comfort of her brothers and parents always near had given Ellamae a sense of trust about people in general and did not school her mind or eyes to deceit and lies. George Forrest was a man who existed for four years in her life and who brought no stories or history and who left two children with her as his only mark on an entire city of people and places. The only known remnants of his life that I can find are a grave, four children, two wives, and a suggestion that his occupation was as an adding machine mechanic and later a radio technician.

The wedding occurred with quite a bit of excitement. A candelabra near the couple saying their vows ignited Ellamae's veil, and memory has it, according to my sources, that it was put out quickly and with no harm to the bride. However, I cannot help but speculate that over the next four or five years of her life, my grandmother wondered if she should have heeded that ominous sign.

There are a few certain facts that I have found out about Ellamae's husband, my grandfather. George Forrest was born on June 5, 1890, and died on February 27, 1950, just four years after Daddy met him. The cause of death on his death certificate is listed as lung cancer, and I learned from his third child, George, that he spent his last days in Rome, Georgia, with his sisters and likely that is why he was buried there. His mother, Catherine Turrentine Chandler, died when he was only six.

******

Miss Gertrude Jones entertained in her home on the day of the Ellis/League wedding and the newspaper article described a typical wedding event of a young lady in society.

ELLIS – LEAGUE

The marriage of Miss Ellamae Ellis. and Mr. George Forrest League, of Shreveport, La., will be solemnized this evening at Centenary Methodist Church, Rev. Mr. Blitch is officiating. MISS GERTRUDE JONES COMPLIMENTS MISS ELLAMAE ELLIS. Elegant in every detail was the reception with which Miss Gertrude Jones entertained on Tuesday afternoon at her home on Vineville Avenue, in honor of Miss Ellamae Ellis, an attractive bride-elect whose wedding will occur this evening. The entire lower floor of the attractive home of Mr. and Mrs. A.F. Jones was thrown in one, and artistic decorations featuring a beautiful effect in rose and green. Miss Jones was assisted in receiving by Miss Ellamae Ellis, Miss Ethel

Whiteside, Miss Horis Ellis, Miss Sara Snelson, of Bostwick, and Miss Julia Higgison. A bevy of young girls who served included Mattabel Jones, and Aran Hightower, and Doris Huston, Lucille Allman, Mary Jones, Ruth Grubbs, Sara Wright, and Mrs. W.C. Dorsett, and Mrs. Paul Gates presided at the punch bowl, and little Miss Marion Dorsett and Baby Martha Virginia Gates served bonbons. About one hundred and twenty-five young people called during the reception hours. Later in the evening, Miss Jones entertained the bridal party after the rehearsal, with a buffet supper. (newspaper, June 28, 1917).

I found an amazing letter that was written to Susie Ellis soon after her daughter's wedding. The author was Agnes Dodson Choate, the wife of Charles Edward Choate [7](1865-1929) who was a brother of Ellamae's mother. Charles was a very prominent architect/Methodist minister who resided in Atlanta from 1909 until 1925. Uncle Herbert (Herbert Emory Choate) and his wife, Julia (Julia Wilson Choate), lived at 10 Park Lane in Atlanta's Piedmont Park. They had a son, John Roquemore Choate, who only lived a year, and their one daughter, Nell, is mentioned in the letter. From the letter, it also seemed that the brothers lived very close to each other. Agnes and Charles's daughter, Anne Dupree Choate is mentioned in the text.[8]

---

[7] Charles E. Choate (1865-1929), New Georgia Encyclopedia, n.georgiaencyclopedia.org.

[8] Anne Dupree (Choate) Dodd, (1907-2000)www.Wikitree.com.

Saturday A.M., July 1917

My Dear Susie, (Susan Choate Ellis)

I have thought so much about you. I want to write and tell you a little about your daughter to cheer your heart. We certainly did enjoy her little visit and she is the sweetest, prettiest, and the most charming girl I know. I have realized what a gem you gave away. Looking at it from the mother's standpoint, it is a tragedy to rear a girl and have her turn out to your liking and then when you can put her on her own responsibility and just enjoy her comes a man to rob you of her, and the world thinks it is the natural thing, but the mother's heart is crying and no one can fill that place. It is a consolation to you to know that her husband adores her. He cannot keep his eyes off her. His every thought is for her. Mr. Choate [Susie's brother and Ellamae's uncle] met them at the station and sent them out, as he was too pressed for time to return with them. Anne Dupree [Uncle Charles Choate's and Agnes's daughter] waited at the carline to escort them over to the house and I met them on the sidewalk. Breakfast was waiting for them and they spent the morning around the house and in their room resting before luncheon. They, Anne Dupree, and Margaret Wade [?] walked over into Piedmont Park and Mr. League took some pictures. They rested in their room till time for their ride with Julia (Uncle Herbert Choate's wife) at five in her new machine. I could not go as I was looking for Hattie and Mr. Chick for dinner. Anne Dupree took my place making five with the driver. They had a lovely drive through Druid Hills and the prettiest parts of the city and returned at seven in time for dinner, just as the other bride and groom arrived. We all had a jolly dinner party. The table was decorated for the occasion with pink and white roses and ferns, candelabra with pink shades and a dainty individual, artificial bridal bouquet of white roses in paper cases and tied with white satin ribbon at each place. Herbert Choate came in and sat with us before we finished and had cream and cake. Anne Dupree thought we had lots of fun. She certainly enjoyed the brides. It was all new to her. She asked me yesterday if Ellamae's other beaux had their feelings hurt when she decided to marry Mr. League, but she said they might as well have their feelings hurt as him. She surprised me and them at the luncheon by breaking a silence with, "Do you want any children?" and repeated it. He answered, "Certainly we do." After dinner, we all went on the front porch and Herbert insisted on our sitting on their porch and listening to the victrola, so we all went over. Nell (Herbert & Julia's daughter) went out as we went in, and she ran over a few minutes before dinner to speak to Ellamae when they were all out in the pergola. As we were enjoying the music and the breeze, I remarked, "What could be more enjoyable than this music and this breeze?" and Mr. League said, "And the right one by your side."

Hattie and Mr. Chick went back to The Ansley at ten. We all walked over to the car with them and came home. I told Ellamae to sleep late as possible yesterday morning, as Julia invited them and me to ten o'clock breakfast. They got well rested here for the rest of their journey. I fixed Ellamae's traveling skirt. I evened it with my skirt marker and bound the hem as it was and stitched it. You had so much to think of. It is a wonder you got through with it. Ellamae said you were in bed the day of the wedding and slept none the night before. Wish you could have been here with them. I don't know why I did not suggest your coming. You could have enjoyed the quiet and rested from responsibilities.

Yesterday, we had breakfast with Julia and Nell at ten. Nell was on a rampage. She is a freelancer and will not stand interference, but Julia holds her own as far as she can. We passed a little tiff between Nell and her mother off pleasantly and had a very enjoyable breakfast. After eating, Nell danced and sang some for us. Ellamae said she thought Nell the cutest thing she ever saw. She is very attractive but spoiled absolutely. I told her at the table if she were mine, I would put her across my lap and spank her and then lock her up until she could behave. She always has a ready answer. I am expecting to keep my daughter away from boarding school if that is the effect. This of course does not to go any further as Herbert dotes on Nell.

I went to the station with Mr. League and Ellamae and the train was one hour and forty-five minutes late, so we walked uptown to a picture show and got back in ample time. He bought her a nice box of Norris candy and said he tried to get Nunnally's and she very tactfully replied, "I like Norris's better." I told her that he would be happy when he got her to himself away from relatives, and she said, "Relatives are not in my way." She said she had the time of her life on this visit. She is so modest; we all fell in love with her. I told him that he would never know what it meant to you and her brothers to give her up. I waved them out of sight at the station. Her hat and suit are so stylish and becoming. Her bridal bouquet is down in the hall minus the ribbons.

Lots of love to you and I want you to run over and see us real soon.

  Love to all,

Agnes (letter from Agnes Choate to Susie Choate Ellis, July 1917)

******

Herbert Emory Choate, his wife, Julia, and daughter, Nell, will later play a huge role in Ellamae's story. Herbert was a very affluent businessman and a longtime resident of Atlanta. Clearly, the wedding trip got off to a smashing start, as described by Agnes in her letter to Susie Ellis in an effort to give her comfort concerning her daughter's marriage.

It is likely that the two mentioned young brides were wearing skirts that were to their ankles and were showing their stylish heels that had replaced the high-buttoned boots.

The Great War had a big influence on fashion in that the tunic had replaced some frills and clothes became more practical. The bright colors of the earlier years gave way to more drab and natural colors. The hats were close to the head and jewelry less flashy. [9]

Mr. League, or George Forrest, sounds like an adoring groom eager to get off on good footing to his young bride's family. I know very little of the next few months or where they traveled or what went wrong, but things did go terribly wrong. My guess is that they were in Shreveport, at least for a time, because I found another letter from Ellamae's father addressed to George Forrest, suggesting that things had gone south very early into the marriage. It reads:

Macon, Ga
January 11, 1918
Shreveport, La.

Mr. G.F. League,
*   The first knowledge of any difference between you and Ellamae that I had was when she received your, well, I won't say letter, but command of December 21st. You must have known from the first she would not be there for Xmas. She came to stay a month and it was her full intention to return at the end of the month. But as soon as she made known to me the man you have proven to be, I could not trust her that distance with you again. You seem to be*

[9] https://bellatory.com/fashion-industry/Women-and-Fashion-of-the-World-War-I-Era-Clothing-1914-1920:1-27.

absolutely void of any conception of a man's duty to his wife.

Your wife is your companion and not a servant or slave. She has the same rights and privileges as the husband. You are not her boss. Neither is she your boss. She has the same right to consideration that you have. You had a special invitation here at Christmas, and if you had wanted to be fair to your wife and everybody concerned, you would have made an effort to come and all enjoy Christmas together. Edward (Ellamae's oldest brother) was here possibly for the last time. As for any explanation, you are just wasting your time and material. I know far better than you do. You forget I lived with her eighteen years and you have been with her for only five months. I believe in the start Ellamae may have some love for you and, with kindness and kind treatment, it would have grown stronger but instead you criticized and found fault with everything she did and abused her and threatened to send her home and now want to tell me that you loved her? You don't love anything or anybody. You are just selfish to the core, and I don't want to hear any of your conditions.

Ellamae is home now, where she is welcome. Love and kindness will be her [illegible]. You will have to show yourself a man before you can get her for a wife again.

Another letter I found is from Ellamae's dear Aunt Ef (Ethel Choate Taylor) dated Saturday morning, January 12, 1918.

"Now what's done is did! A lot of time could be wasted by all of us who are deeply concerned about your happiness by wishing that we could have foreseen what has just happened. But there is only one sensible thing to do and that is for everybody to get so busy that there will be no time for brooding. Just be thankful that the climax came as soon as it did. You are still merely a child and everybody knows you are a pure, innocent child and your life and happiness lies before you. I'm rather glad you are in Macon where everybody knows and loves you, though I know that for a while it will be very, very hard for you. You can be sure that the real people will understand and give you a square deal."

Her next four pages are too priceless to omit, and they give me a glimpse of the advice and love surrounding Ellamae in her eighteenth year of life. These words were apparently played in her mind again and again as she set out to take on a man's profession.

"There is nothing in the world that helps what ails you like work. I mean real, genuine, systematic work. I don't know what your plans are, but it would make me feel so satisfied to know that you are actively at work for our country in some capacity. I think it would be wonderful for you to have the Red

Cross nurse training. And it is my opinion that every man, woman, and child in America is going to have to roll up their sleeves and pitch in before this fight is over. I am so thankful for the privilege of having a small part in saving democracy. It would be a horrible thing for Germany to win – too horrible to contemplate. The thought of it makes your troubles and mine fade into insignificance. I don't know whether you and Susie have joined the Red Cross or not, but if not, please do. If I could only make you see things as I see them. We are in danger, not as individuals but as a nation and we must get busy. It's time to put aside selfishness and the pursuit of pleasure as the one aim in life and get busy and do not do our bit but our ALL to keep old glory flappin'. This doesn't sound like me, does it? Well, it isn't me. The Kaiser has made another woman of me and I am tingling to fight him with his own weapons. If you haven't read or heard of the horrible atrocities that are being committed at his direction, read up and thank God that you are an American woman and then get busy. It's all bosh about the woman who stays at home and sees their loved ones go are the greatest heroes. Nothing heroic about that. They do it because they can't help themselves. It's the women who spend every second of their spare time doing something to make those who go more comfortable or else take a man's place in the office so he can go to the front. Not handing myself a bouquet either. I didn't feel this way until I was actually in the service. I think it is as much our duty to observe meatless days and wheatless days, etc. as it is to knit and roll bandages. The chances are very strong in favor of my being out of the service before the war is over because of physical inability, but I'll still feel just as I do now and hope I will always be able to at least knit.

I'm just crazy to hear from you again and know just what developments have taken place and what your plans are.

And now I must tell you how much I enjoyed the New Year's box of candy and cake and nuts. I got it before I crawled out of bed on New Year's morning, and it certainly was a beautiful beginning to the New Year 1918. The candy and cakes were grand and you know my sentiments about pecans, especially when the meats are picked out for me. Some little candy maker you are, and I guess you must have had a finger in the cake too, which was so good that I gobbled it all up myself with the exception of a very small piece.

I wrote Florine this morning, but I didn't mention your affairs except to say that I supposed that Mr. League would be drafted. The aforementioned package contained three pairs of much-needed Theodore's, some homemade sausage, and a glass of jelly. Had the sausage for lunch today and they were fine, as I guess you know, and the jelly I'm saving against the time I go to light housekeeping.

Keep a stiff upper lip and don't forget that I would do anything in this world to make you happy. Loads of love to each one of you,

Aunt Ef (letter from Ethel Choate Taylor to Ellamae
E. League, January 12, 1918)

Aunt Ef was living in Washington, DC, at the time, and was in the navy. She was a sister of Susie Ellis and, I believe, had been married at some point because her last name was no longer Choate. Perhaps her husband was deceased. Many years after the war, she joined the Sisters of Saint Joseph of Carondelet as Sister Margaret Mary Taylor and died when I was a young girl. I believe that it was in 1960 and she was at that time at St. Joseph's Home for Boys[10] in Washington, Georgia. During her years as a nun, she visited Ellamae in her home in Macon and was required then to always travel with another nun. I remember some of her visits and her twinkly blue eyes that were always joy-filled.

******

This sheds new light on the theory that George Forrest was in the military and stationed, perhaps at Camp Wheeler. It begs the question that he was trying to avoid the military. On a census I saw that was taken almost eighteen years later, George Forrest filled in his occupation as a radio technician. Though I am certain he fathered at least four children, he only listed two, and those were from his second marriage.

---

[10] Angelique M. Richardson, CA, Archivist, Office of Archives and Records, Archdiocese of Atlanta.

Too many question marks and only records and old letters to fill in the blanks!

Clearly, just five months into their marriage, Ellamae and George Forrest hit a huge roadblock. An eighteen-year-old girl and a twenty-seven-year-old man marry and flee her home and family to Shreveport on a train. Blank months. Was he abusive and critical in the way she reported to her father, or was she spoiled and not willing to be a dutiful wife? At any rate, Ellamae returned to Macon alone to have Christmas with her parents.

The war was foremost on everyone's mind, and uncertainty and fear may have felt tenfold to a young girl so far from home for the first time in her life. What were her days like in Shreveport, and did George Forrest still adore her, or was he trying to mold her into a submissive wife?

The world was aflame even after Armistice and the Spanish Flu Pandemic of 1918. It left Americans skeptical and confused, which was the wild, live-for-the-moment mindset that brought on the roaring twenties. It was a whole new attitude for America in so many ways. The risqué look, the music, and the fashion all spoke of the effects of the years they had survived.

Here the mystery grows deeper because I do know that at some point, George Forrest returned to Macon and he and Ellamae lived with her parents as husband and wife for just shy of four years. Jean League was born on March 20, 1919, and my dad, Joseph Choate League, was born on March 27, 1921. In the year between my aunt's and dad's births, Ellamae's parents gave birth to their second daughter, Marjorie Ellis, so there was definitely some harmony for a time. I located a 1920 census that listed Ellamae as twenty and George Forrest as twenty-nine. The address was her parents' home on Rembert Avenue, and George Forrest noted his occupation as a bookkeeper in the railroad industry.

Family lore has it that soon after Marjorie, Susie and Joe's sixth child was born, Susie's health suffered. She had asthma and would later suffer much pain from arthritis in her hip. Joe adored his wife and decided to move her, young Dilworth, and Marjorie to Miami. No one is clear about the sequence of events, but most likely the final split occurred before the family moved. What dark event happened is likely to remain buried with the characters, but very soon after my dad's birth, while he was a small infant, Joseph Ellis banished George Forrest from the house, the city, and from ever seeing Ellamae or their children again.

Sometime after leaving his family in Macon, George Forrest landed in New York, where he met and married his second wife. He fathered two more sons, George Herbert League (July 8, 1929 – October 9, 2018) and Walter Graham League (December 2, 1930 – January 30, 1990). After the brief and awkward meeting in Warner Robins with their mutual father, Daddy never saw either of his younger half-brothers again, but the story doesn't end there.

In October of 2016, while trying to learn more about my mystery grandfather, I discovered that George, the oldest of his two sons from his second marriage, who was about eight years younger than my father, was still alive and lived with his wife in a retirement community in Florida. I stayed awake for two nights laboring over a letter that I would write to him, then eighty-seven years old, and how I might word it. So many questions filled my head and it took me weeks to refine my words into a letter that I thought would not intrude on or disturb this man's privacy. After several weeks, I was satisfied that I could mail it, and I included my address, email, and phone number. Barely a week passed, and one afternoon my phone rang.

"Is this Cheri?" a sweet voice asked.

"Yes," I replied.

"This is George League's wife, and in all our years, George and I have never been so moved by anything as your letter. He's right here and he wants to talk to you."

Just nine months before this phone call, my father had died at age ninety-four, just one month and five days before his ninety-fifth birthday. My mother, his bride of almost seventy-three years, had preceded him by ten months, and though Daddy was still driving and very sharp just weeks before his death, his lonely heart had done his bidding and taken him to heaven.

Daddy and I had always been close, and to make this connection so soon after his death was beyond 'emotional' for me.

"How old are you?" he asked.

"Seventy-one," I said, choking on the lump in my throat but letting the tears run down my face.

"Well, I am eighty-seven, and don't you die before I can meet you."

George went on to tell me that he had a stroke many years earlier and that it had affected his memory. He had very little recollection of his life as a boy and of his father, my grandfather. He was not certain that he knew enough to help me with my book, but he said he would love to meet me. In September, my sister, brother, and I drove down and spent three days with George and his wife. We became family. Just a little over a year ago, George died at home with his loving wife at his side, and I lost an uncle and my dad's half-brother, and my life is richer for the short time I had with him.

George did not remember meeting my father on that day in 1946. Maybe his father never told him he had a half-brother. Maybe he never told him or Walter that he was married before. His younger brother, Walter, had passed away many years prior, and George's distant memory was gone. So many gifts came from knowing my Uncle George, and he did shed a little light, but the details that had remained in Uncle George's memory of his father were not good ones – in fact, quite the contrary. The day young George turned eighteen, July 18, 1947, he enlisted in the Air Force and returned home just long enough to tell his brother and gather his things. He never said goodbye to his father, and the best he could recall, he never saw him again. Three years later, George Forrest League died. Uncle George did recall that he and Walter had been awarded to their father because their mother was not able to support them. His words to me about that stung!

"Your dad was the lucky one. He had a mother who could take care of him."

Though he lacked specifics, George had bad memories connected to his father, but he recalled his mother very lovingly.

Chapter 4

*"Sometimes when you are in a dark place, you
think you have been buried, but you've actually been
planted. BLOOM."*

CHRISTINE CAINE [11]

1928

Joe League

Momma's hand was gloved, so I couldn't really feel it or
take much comfort from it. Jean was smiling and excited to
ride the train and at the prospect of living with Margie, but
I was worried about sharing a room with two girls. Well, I
consoled myself, Grand Joe will be sure I get a square deal.
Momma said Miami was a swell place to live, and it was
summer all the time there, so I could play outside from
breakfast to supper.

"It won't be that long," Ellamae promised as she turned
her little passengers over to the Ladies Aide lady, who

---

[11] Christine Caine, *6 Life Changing Quotes from Christine Caine-
Odyssey*, www.theodysseyonline.com.

looked capable enough. Ellamae had packed sweets and sandwiches for the children to share on the long train ride to show her appreciation. She had time to tell Jean and Joe a few more stories of what it would be like in France and the ship she would be sailing on and how the time would pass quickly until she collected them back home to Macon.

The entire platform seemed to tremble and a booming roar filled my ears and there was a very oily, steamy smell as the enormous train filled the station. The platform exploded with small ladders falling out of doorways and dark red-coated men assisting passengers off the train. So much luggage appeared that I was feeling a little afraid that I might get swept away with someone's suitcase and Momma wouldn't see me. Mother's gloved hand disappeared and suddenly she was waving and another gloved hand of the Ladies Aide lady grabbed mine and pulled me up the stairs. The train was very crowded in the aisles, but we didn't have far to go before the nice lady said we had arrived at our seats. When I sat down, I was filled with relief to find that Jean was right behind me and looked as scared as I felt. I would not cry, for if I did, Jean might as well, and then there'd be no stopping us. Mother promised that Grand Susie and Grand Joe would be at our final stop, and she had never steered us wrong, so I just held on to that thought.

My appetite sort of vanished for the first part of the trip, but just the smell of Momma on the things she had packed made me feel a little better. We had been told that at one stop, the Ladies Aide lady would get off the train and a new lady would come on to finish the trip with us. A second package of sweets was provided for her. I sure hoped that

that part of the trip would work out and that Jean and I would be able to refrain from eating all of the goodies. I didn't want Momma getting any bad reports.

The train ride was a real adventure. One of my favorite spots was the area between the cars where they were coupled. At first, it felt real scary to stand there between the doors because it was bumpy and swayed a lot and it wasn't as warm as the rest of the train. It was a lot noisier there, too, because you could hear the train swooshing along the tracks. After a few times, I started to not feel scared. The lavatories were really first-rate, too. The constant rocking and aiming at such a small toilet took some practice. I was sure happy that the Ladies Aide lady stood outside because when I would try to open the door, it would swing back fast and slam closed before I could get out.

It seemed like a long time since we'd told Momma goodbye when we finally ended our train journey. She was right about it being summer all the time in Miami. I hardly had to unpack my sweater, and Grand Susie said all she ever did was wash our clothes. She had Margie's clothes to wash anyway, so it was not like we were too much trouble, or that's what she always said.

It seemed like relatives were always visiting at my grandparent's house. Ice came every day instead of every other, and it seemed like the beds always felt damp. Living with two girls was not so bad, and Grand Joe did have my back when the girl stuff got to me. It turned out that Margie liked to play a lot of the same things as I did, and Jean just went along to not be trouble. All in all, Margie was just as excited as we were when a letter or a postcard came from Momma telling us about her classes and promising that she had stories to tell us when she got home. She said that there were only two other ladies in her class. The pictures on the postcards looked like places in another world and from another time. I really didn't love looking at them because it made me feel like she was so far away, and maybe it wasn't really her and maybe she would never get home. Grand Susie always put the cards out on the parlor table with the pictures showing so we could all go look at them whenever we wanted, but I definitely preferred letters.

I learned about some new things while we lived there, like hurricanes. My grandparents' house was not real close to the beach, but we felt them really bad when they came. We had no warning at all except common sense, and people there seemed to have a lot of that when it came to the weather. My Uncle Eugene had a small boat, and he spent a lot of time running back and forth to the bay to check on it and 'batten it down,' which was another new thing I learned all about. Since I could not swim too well yet, Uncle Eugene would tie some rope around my waist and tell me to stay close when we went down to the docks.

Grand Joe took care of us when things got so scary in the hurricane. It rained so hard that pots and pans sat all around to catch the drips coming through the roof. Grand Joe had me help him nail the kitchen table to the doorway because a palm tree had flown right through it. My grandmother was crazy with worry because Eugene and Dilworth had gone to batten down the boat and didn't return for a very long time. The storm showed no signs of calming. We had no understanding about the eyes of hurricanes back then, and we later learned that the uncles had been stranded

61

on a bridge hanging on for all they were worth. Jean and I really missed Momma that day.

I had some stationery that Momma got me, and it had trains on it and lines so I could write straight. Sometimes I wrote to her and put it in the envelope, but I am not sure my grandmother ever mailed them because Momma never mentioned them when she wrote.

******

Ellamae

The walk back to the car where Bill waited to drive me home seemed surreal. The children's faces planted like a photograph in my brain. Twice, I stumbled into strangers hurrying along the platform and I was hoping to get to Bill's arms before I would hear the train fade away.

Before now, life always felt certain. Even during the war, I always had a sense that it would end, that life would resume, and that things would be the same. Today is different. This feels even scarier than leaving my marriage. Of that I was certain, but this feels like something different. In less than a week, I will broad a train to New York with Nell and then a ship to France. Anything could happen. I might never see my children again. I feel like I am going through all the motions of my plan, but that my plan feels like it is for someone else. On paper, it all seems so right.

Bill was waving when I finally pushed through the doors of the terminal and I was so afraid that if I stopped moving, my legs might collapse. This was a feeling that I never anticipated, and even though I packed the children with great care and double-checked my lists, I am overwhelmed with the sense that I have failed them.

He seemed to know that I was teetering and immediately began a litany of reassurances.

"They looked happy and full of excitement. Joe was fascinated with the train, and they will have each other. It's an adventure they will never forget. The year will be gone before you know it."

Walking into my apartment, now devoid of anything childish, brought all the doubt back. This feeling that I have to keep moving hit me again and I reminded myself of all the things left on my to-do list before my own departure. Again, I will just keep moving because it is too late to turn back the train swooshing south.

I am wasting time thinking this way. This is just the next intersection along the road, and to do this takes me closer to what I must do to provide for us. This is my moment to seize and not run from – My moment to build a real life for us. Today is today, and I will use it wisely.

Chapter 5

1991

Ellamae

I can never hear Mary Jane coming. She is so uncomfortable in my house, or so it seems to me. She walks and speaks quietly as though it might make her invisible. I love her. I always have. Just so out of her comfort zone, I think. Now, forty-four years or so in Macon and yet she feels like she is living in Joe's world, not her own. She loves me, too, and has always included me and treated me lovingly. I never heard her coming until her voice raised just barely above the TV. Naomi must have been surprised, too, because she jumped to turn the television off. After a few quiet questions that I can barely make out, she is off. Mary Jane hates coming now that I am so close. She can't stay because she is fleeing the death scene and feels so inadequate. She is a stranger to sickness, if you can call dying a sickness, and she just can't see me like this.

All the 'drop-ins' are running together for me now, and I am not sure if it is day or night. Turn me over, Naomi, my mind pleads, so I can feel light from the window. I think I am alone now.

My mind is at once settled on things I think are real, and the next minute, somewhere I am sure I have never been. I am sure I am speaking but acutely aware that I cannot make my mouth work. My throat is so dry; I can't even part my lips. I'm in the Grand Opera House, and I am keenly aware of the feel of the velvet fabric on the seat and all the jewel colors, and I have on my ice-blue gown, but I'm the only one there, and I am on the wrong night. I feel scared because how could I have made such a mistake? Maybe I have forgotten other big things or made other big mistakes.

"That's silly, Ellamae," she hears Bill's reassuring voice. "We've been over every detail and it's beautiful. Just sit there and take it all in."

Before she can linger and take in Bill's face and the comfort he gives, *poof!* He is gone and replaced by Delmar.

Poof, again. She's at Mulberry Street Methodist Church, and it's burned out, and she is panting so hard and smells smoke so strongly that she is sure that she has been running. Fragments of this and that are wearing her out. Her breathing feels so labored now, but if she can keep running, she can go farther and farther back and see more and more.

Her big Buick is pulling up beside her, and she feels so relieved and jumps in. Marsha is driving. How great it is to see her, and she looks wonderful, smiling so big, and she's young. They drive for only a few minutes, and they turn onto College Street.

"Turn back, Marsha," Ellamae wills her.

There are no words. Just thinking things seems to work in this new place between life and death. Marsha turns the car around and they are instantly on Waverland Drive.

******

James Barfield wrote for *Macon Magazine* an article entitled: The Grand Duchess of Macon Architecture Left Her Mark on the City, in 1992. He described Ellamae as arriving at a Hollywood-like event honoring her and other 'Grand Dames' of Macon at the Grand Opera House. James described her as petite, blond, with pale blue eyes, and seemingly fragile. She was wearing a long silver-white sheath, and he described her simple, clean lines and elegance.

"A stranger observing Mrs. League's entrance that night might have wondered what had given her that special presence, that aura of dignity and pride. Those who knew of her life, her career, and her achievements had no reason to wonder." [12]

---

[12] James Barfield, *Macon Magazine*, (January – February 1992):31, 33, and 39.

I love sharing someone else's opinion and the last sentence suggests that many knew her life story when none did.

******

September 19, 1928

Ellamae

Standing alone on the deck of the massive SS France,[13] commissioned just a week after the Titanic sank, I am imagining the stories it could tell – romance, intrigue… After all, the captain mentioned that it served as a hospital ship during World War I, so it has seen death and despair, too. Fourteen days now on board and the palace-like décor and its gaudiness is getting old. The announcements last night said to be on deck by 10:00 a.m. to see Lady Liberty come into view as we enter the mouth of the harbor. For US citizens, the process should be fairly easy, and I pray that will be the case. I dreamed of this moment, but now I am more scared than I was when I left.

If I don't miss my train, I'll be in Macon in two more days, and there will be a new office and so much to learn and catch up on, but who am I kidding? What is Bill expecting? What am I expecting? What do I want? I have no answers and can promise nothing…

My children… that scares me, too. Are they happier and better off with Mother and Dad? It's September and I can't start them in school in October, and Mama says I better

---

[13] https://en.wikipedia.org/wiki/SS France (1910).

work it out 'cause she has Margie to worry about. Bill is expecting me to jump right in, but I just have to get my ducks in a row. The apartment is going to need some work, though Bill said he's had someone in to make it ready… I can't think about it or it'll spoil the whole homecoming.

"I'm home," she almost breathed the words. Half the manifest was made up of Americans, so she'd grown accustomed to hearing English again on the long voyage. Soon, she would have a lot more to reacquaint herself to.

Chapter 6

"Peace is the result of retraining your mind to process life as it is, rather than how you think it should be."

WAYNE W. DYER [14]

1921

Susan Dilworth Choate Ellis, Ellamae's mother, was facing a bad dream, or so it felt like to her. At forty-six, she had given birth to her second daughter and sixth child. This time around, motherhood was more difficult for her than for her daughter, Ellamae, who was a mother herself. Young Marjorie Ellis (born March 1920) was one, and her older sister's daughter Jean, born March 20, 1919, was already two. Little Joe, born on March 27, 1921, was an infant and Ellamae was a single mother of two. Because of Susan Ellis's fragile health, her husband, Joe, had made plans to move his family to Miami. The warm climate and a change of scenery would lighten the load. The stress of their oldest

---

[14] Wayne Dyer Quotes and Daily Affirmations: *everydaypower.com.*

daughter's situation likely was the greatest cause of her health problems. It is unclear to me who took care of Ellamae's infant and two-year-old while she went to work, but a young mother, divorced and working outside the home, was an oddity. It is hard for me to imagine how she did it and found time to take correspondence courses, but she did. World War I was a distant memory, but the world was still tumbling. I found a lay-away slip for art supplies and maybe a drawing board, which suggested to me that Ellamae had her sights set very early on. She was juggling so many balls, and I can only guess that her parents had to be helping her financially in those first few years on her own.

Macon was beginning to boom and expand around the railroad. By 1920, Macon had a population of fifty-three thousand, and people were flocking to the cities looking for jobs. In just under twenty years, the population had doubled, and the mostly white residents now included an influx of black people that accounted for forty-three percent of its residents. Sadly, Dixie Klan No. 33 came to Macon in 1919, and fifteen Macon men joined their ranks,[15] a shameful blemish on the city's history.

At this point, obviously, many believed that Macon would continue to grow and flourish because of the railroad. Situated in the center of the state, Macon was a great place to be for some. Industry was exploding and producing products like lumber, textiles, iron, and clay products. The downtown area was busy and vital, and the buildings

---

[15] "The Ku Klux Klan in Macon, 1919-1925," *The Georgia Historical Quarterly*, 62/2, (Summer, 1978), 155 – 168.

reflected an attitude that the surge would continue. Churches were built large and grand, as were department stores and even theaters. Judging it today, one might wonder why young Ellamae decided to part from her family and face life alone when the road looked much smoother if she had chosen to move with her family to Miami. My belief is that somewhere deep in her soul, she knew her life would be conventional and she had a yearning to do more. After all, hadn't she just walked out on 'conventional?'

Rarely did young Ellamae, now only twenty-two, argue with her parents, but her strong head could not be persuaded to leave Macon. Certainly, the family must have believed her choice to remain would prove so difficult that she would come to her senses and join the rest of them in Florida. I doubt that anyone would have put money on her being able to make it on her own. After all, in 1921, what could a woman do to support her family? I wonder if that old letter from her precious Aunt Ef was playing in her mind when Ellamae decided to pursue a man's profession.

Six generations of Ellamae's family on her mother's side had been architects, and her Uncle Charles Edward Choate was actively practicing at the time. Georgia Tech, in Atlanta, would have been the likely path for a Georgia resident, but the school did not admit women at this time. Besides, she had two young children and needed an income. Atlanta was out of the question unless she had help.

The architectural firm of Elliott Dunwody and William F. Oliphant went out on a limb and hired Ellamae to do office work. She had an apartment at Katherine Court Apartments and was really on her own.

William F. Oliphant was just home from France and refreshed from his studies at Ecole des Beau-Arts in Fountainebleau.[16] Bill had remained in France following the First World War, where he fought on the front lines, I think as a courier. When his duty and the war ended, he stayed to further his studies and clear his head of the death and despair he'd witnessed. He was back in Macon and setting up his practice when this young apprentice made it clear that she wanted to learn all that she could.

Bill Oliphant could see Ellamae's determination and willingness to work hard. Maybe her architectural bloodline impressed him or maybe her beauty and guile. Whatever it was, he encouraged her to take correspondence courses from Beaux-Arts in New York, and soon she was availing herself of all the tools of the trade in the office and was listening in and soaking up all that she could. Two small children drove her to work to provide for them, but they lacked for a mother who was present. During this time in her life, it seemed that Ellamae's passion changed from simply needing to provide for her children to a passion for architecture. Some old letters to Ellamae from Bill Oliphant made it clear that she had become a team member and quite indispensable in the office. Bill was a huge influence on her, and from my father, I gleaned that he was more. Daddy and Jean were old enough to notice his constant presence and their attraction. Daddy felt that they would have married had it not been for Bill's early death. In some of the paperwork that I found after Daddy died were those

---

[16] *The Macon Telegraph*, CVII/20, Monday Morning, April 3, 1933.

personal papers that had been in Ellamae's attic prior to her death. Many were Bill's from the war and his fourteen months fighting and later studying in France, which was prior to them knowing each other. Why would he leave such personal things in her care? Many photographs from his time in France, both during the war and after, remained with her. There were several letters between them while she was in France many years later and a few while she was traveling for business related to the firm. They have a personal and sweet tone, though not overtly romantic by today's standards. Deep affection and respect were present in their exchanges, so I can only deduce that romance was present. My father also told me that his mother never seriously considered marriage after Bill died.

Bill had grown up in Macon and attended Lanier High School and then gone to Georgia Tech (about 1909) to study architecture. He was eight years ahead of Ellamae, so I would guess that they didn't know each other before she went to work for him.

Meanwhile, Ellamae's mother's brother, Herbert Emory Choate (one of the uncles she visited on her wedding trip), had become a successful businessman in Atlanta. Remember his spoiled daughter, Nell? Nell had, by now, completed her education in boarding school and was a talented artist. It was her desire to go to France and study art, so this was when the tide turned in Ellamae's favor. Nell's father and mother decided it would not be wise to send Nell abroad without a proper chaperone, so they asked Ellamae to be her escort. The young women would sail to France and stay a year, and Ellamae would be compensated by taking courses herself. The deal was sealed.

Since Ellamae's mother had a young daughter who fell in age right between her own two, her parents agreed to keep Jean and Joe who were now eight and six. It's hard to imagine how hard that year must have been for the two young children, and the truth is that it really drew on longer because when Ellamae returned, she imposed on her parents for a good while longer to keep the children in Florida as she resettled.

I know very little of Ellamae's year in Fontainebleau, other than she was one of three women in her class, but she sailed home alone on the SS France in September of 1928. Nell had met a young man whom she later married, and she went on to return to the states and make a name for herself as a fine watercolorist and painter.

Ellamae returned with lots of souvenirs and, having been heavily influenced by the Bauhaus school of design, an impressive résumé. In her absence, Dunwody and Oliphant had split, and Bill joined Claude Shelverton, whom Ellamae went to work for. This alliance was short-lived and became just Oliphant. A young budding architect named Delmar Warren also worked in the office, but neither he nor Ellamae were registered. An apprentice had to sit exams and have had a degree or ten years of practical experience in the profession to be registered. Both she and Delmar could work on projects, but they could not take on new projects without someone in the office being registered.

Jean was brought to Macon to be with her mother and begin school. Ellamae pressed on her parents to keep Joe a little longer, as she felt ill-equipped to manage a very active boy of seven. It is painful for me to imagine what might have gone through my dad's mind when his mother sent for his sister but not him. What it conjures in me can only pale next to that of a seven-year-old.

My father told me a heart-wrenching story of his memory of that time.

According to him, his grandparents felt put-upon and thought that their daughter had taken advantage of them. Their oldest son, Edward, was going to travel in a car to Macon and bring young Joe to his mother to surprise her. After days of travel and riding in an open car, they arrived at the Grand Building in Macon where Ellamae worked. Edward had stopped on the way in and acquired a large box for young Joe to hide in, and they had made a plan that when his mother came out to the car, my dad would pop out yelling, "Surprise!" They rehearsed it, and Edward set up clues so Daddy would know the exact moment to spring. Right on cue, he popped out of the box, but instead of shouts of glee and hugs and kisses, Daddy remembers that his mother was furious and berated her brother at great length for thinking it was great fun.

Daddy was enrolled at Whittle School along with his sister, Jean. Whittle was just barely two blocks from their apartment and an easy walking distance. A vivid memory of my dad is that his mother never darkened the school door, not even when he was awarded the Legionnaire Award in the seventh grade. It was always obvious in Daddy's recollections that he missed his mother's presence in his life, especially as a young boy. His detailed memories of these kinds of events spoke loudly of pain to my ears, but he just as strongly defended his mother by proclaiming excuses for her. Her need to provide or the Depression or his favorite, which was, "She just didn't know what to do with a boy." There was no question that a price was paid for a career mother when career mothers were not the norm. Also, the fact that she had grown up with four brothers made Daddy's favorite declaration invalid.

******

The three young children, Jean, Joe, and Margie, spent a good part of the summer of 1930 with Uncle Herbert and Aunt Julia in Atlanta and wrote many letters to their mother in Macon. The general theme was of the wonderful spoilin' they were getting from the Choates, with lots of watermelon and frequent ice cream cones following rides in the park, including their first experience with a flavor called 'rainbow.' Best of all, all three of them had learned to swim and had contests holding their breaths and staying under at the Piedmont Park Pool. Each letter, be it from Jean or Joe, ended in, *"Please write. I miss you."*

Despite the confections and glorious car rides and adventures of summer, they longed for their mother.

Ellamae was busy in the office and was now integral to its projects and fully functioning as an architect. Then, Bill got sick. The diagnosis was pernicious enema. Today, it is an easily curable disease, but then, he was hospitalized and given six transfusions and was scheduled for the seventh. There was nothing to be done to stop the progression of the disease, and on April 2, 1933, Bill died.[17] Did he leave

---

[17] Ibid.

Ellamae with dying wishes for her to carry on? Did he tell her to be bold and finish their work?

There was an office full of projects and work to be finished. In October 1933, six months after Bill Oliphant's death, Ellamae went to Atlanta to sit the state board exams. She became registered and opened her own office, and young Delmar Warren went with her.

The Great Depression was cranking up and would change life for every person in America. Certainly, the poor were the hardest hit. Their reserves were nonexistent, and they could not keep their farms from drying up and manufacturing jobs were hard to find. Many people lived in encampments called 'hoovervilles'[18] with other hobos and traveled from place to place in search of work. Black employment dropped to five percent. Breadlines sprang up to try and meet the most basic needs of the people. Franklin Roosevelt promoted government programs and imposed rationing. He recruited six million defense workers and drafted another six million soldiers, including women and blacks. Some of these government contracts provided the work that kept Ellamae's office afloat. One of her earliest commissions came from the Federal Works Progress Administration for the reconstruction of Macon's earliest building, the 1806 Fort Hawkins blockhouse. It remains a major landmark in the city.

Jean and Daddy were fourteen and twelve at the time and had six years previously moved to College Street to a larger apartment with their mother. College Street was a

---

[18] The Eleanor Roosevelt Papers Project, Department of History of the George Washington University, https://www.2gwu.edu/erpapers/teachinger/glossary/great-depression.com.

social center and provided a grand education for teenagers. Some of Macon's finest homes and residents lived along the street of historic homes, and they had friends galore. It was on College Street that Daddy first met Ira King.

My dad felt that he wore short, in his words, 'little Lord Fauntleroy pants' long after it was appropriate and that his mother had no idea what to do with a boy. Jean was polished and social and all a mother could want. He, on the other hand, needed a father and someone to show him the ropes. Daddy started hiding long pants and clothes more to his liking at the house of Ira King, who would not only care for Daddy but educate him far beyond his years.

Ira worked for a family that lived next door to the large house where Ellamae rented an apartment. Behind the house was something that Daddy described as little more than a shed which had no heat other than a fireplace. Daddy said it did have running water but that it often froze in the winter. Ira's wife was named Beauty, but according to Daddy, she wasn't. There was plenty of love to go around, even beyond their many children who had the most wonderful names you can imagine. I so wish Daddy could speak from his grave to tell me their names again so I could list them all here. The only ones that stuck in my mind are a daughter named Toot-a-loo, whom Daddy called Toot or Sista, and twin sons named Ike and Mike. I know that Beauty died in childbirth at some point, and Ira raised the children on his own after that.

Kids went to the Saturday matinee for ten cents and that bought them four hours of entertainment. The main feature might be a serial, like *The Perils of Pauline* or *Our Gang*, or a western, then a newsreel and various short-subject films. Talkies came on the scene when Joe and Jean were children, and they remembered stars such as Tom Mix and William Hart. In those days, no food or drinks were allowed in the theater and could only be had at intermission. [19]

Houses had clotheslines outback and washboards on the back porch because there were no washing machines. Only very fine homes had electricity, and most still had gaslight or kerosene lanterns. Clothes were cotton, wool, or silk, and shoes were leather except for Keds, which were only worn by boys. There was no plastic, and telephones were made out of a very hard rubber substance called gutta-percha. [20]

It cost a dime to ride the streetcar and a dime to make a phone call. When you picked up the phone, an operator said, "Number please?" Most phones had party lines, which meant you shared a line and other people could and would listen in to your conversations. Ellamae had a rare private line, and it cost her $2.75 a month. A long-distance call or a telegram came usually because someone had died or worse. [21]

Every boy needs a dog, and Daddy would have never had the experience if not for Ira. I am not sure that Daddy ever knew where King came from, but Ira produced a white German Shepherd that became a constant companion for Daddy. Not only did he love that dog, but Daddy really loved Ira.

Daddy carried so many hobbies into adulthood, and most of them stemmed from the skills Ira taught him, like

---

[19] Letter from Joseph C. League, Sr. to Bob Tribble, *The Wilkinson County News*.
[20] Ibid.
[21] Ibid.

whittling. Daddy could take a piece of wood and carve it into almost anything. Like Ira, he could take almost anything apart and put it back correctly.

What most young boys learned from their dads, my daddy learned at Ira's heels. He made arrows with arrowheads out of coins he put on the train tracks to flatten, and likely, he learned how to drive from Ira. Add to the good was also the bad, like cock fights. College Street was close to the Ocmulgee River and Ira would take his young white friend to the banks in the night, amongst all the black faces. There were likely other things not so laudable, but there is no question that Daddy would have been a different man without the tutorage of Ira King. One thing about Ira was that he was always there, or so it seemed. When Daddy returned to Macon after his flight training, Ira had moved to Detroit according to neighbors, and though he tried, Daddy never saw him again. This seeming abandonment probably had a greater impact on his life than did that of his own father. After all, he had no memory of his dad.

In a letter from my dad to my mom, he wrote of his young years on College Street and how he recalled the Depression:

"Things – acquiring things is important to me. I never get enough – probably because of the way I grew up. As a child, we never had things. Even toys. I made most of mine. I have a feeling of success and accomplishment when I acquire something valuable. I know you don't understand that, but I will probably never change.

From the time I was eight or nine, I was taught that there's almost nothing I cannot do if someone else can do it. Someone may do it better than I do, but I can do it well enough to get by, and some things I can do better than others. When I was a kid, I made all my own toys – bows and arrows, pop guns, rubber guns, swords, skate mobiles, tree houses, and my first tennis racquet... It was an old one that I found that I restrung myself with some heavy fishing line. When I was thirteen, Henry Kendall gave me a cheap, single-shot twenty-two rifle. It wasn't new, but I thought it was. It was the greatest thing I ever had. I could buy a box of twenty-two shorts (fifty cartridges) for sixteen cents (if I could scrap up sixteen cents). Ira King gave me a 'hunting knife.' I didn't own a pocketknife. Mother knew nothing about boys. For Christmas, I always got clothes. When I graduated from Whittle (1933), I won the American Legion Medal, so I got a Boy Scout uniform to wear when the medal was presented. It was the only one I ever had, but many scouts never had one. I never had any tools because there was none of any kind in our apartment. The closest thing I ever had to a tool was that hunting knife, and I used it for more things than Tarzan did. I had one bicycle in my life and it was one size smaller than full size. Jean got one also and never used hers, so when I wore mine completely out, I took over hers. No boy would be caught dead on a girl's bike, so I tied a broomstick across the top, seat post to front post, and painted it blue with blue ink

so it would look like a boy's bike, or so I hoped.
Walter Grace's mother saw what it was and said so.
Walter had a new Iver Johnson, so when I became
an adult and could buy things for myself, I did.
Maybe too many things, but I enjoy all of them."
(notes from Joseph C. League Sr. to his wife, Mary
Jane)

******

Ellamae had an aunt named Augusta Choate, who built
and directed Choate School in Boston (1920–1947.) [22]
Choate was a finishing school for girls located on Beacon
Street, in Brookline, Massachusetts. Jean graduated from
Macon's A.L. Miller High School in 1937, just as the
Depression was winding down. Jean's daughter tells me
that she doesn't know why it was decided that Jean would
not go straight to college. Perhaps Ellamae felt she needed
more maturity, or maybe Aunt Augusta Choate encouraged
Jean and her mother that travel north would be best under
her tutelage, but Jean boarded a train in the fall and attended
Choate for a year. Being always an excellent student, Jean
went from Choate to Radcliffe, but for a year or two, she
continued to live at Choate with her aunt. Simultaneously,
she completed her undergraduate degree at Radcliffe and
her graduate degree in design and architecture from Harvard
over the next six years, finishing in 1944. In that same year,
Jean joined her mother's practice in Macon.

---

[22] "Historical Images of Brookline," by Brookline Historical
Society, https://patch.com/users/brookline-historical-society,
September 1, 2017.

At sixteen, Joe was still at Lanier High School and enjoying his friends, girlfriends, driving, and dancing. His neighbors down the street were the Graces, and they had two daughters and a son, Walter. Ruth Grace was one of Jean's best friends, and the other youngest daughter, Agnes (Aggie), was Daddy's favorite dance partner, at least until he met my mother. Ruth left for Vassar the same year Jean headed to Boston. There are many letters between them that tell how their friendship continued.

Young Joe and Aggie Grace were quite famous in local circles for their dancing skills. Joe and his friends spent many nights at Lakeside Park dancing the night away. He was in a high school fraternity and a fun companion for his mother, but he was also a boy who was left to his own devices too often. Daddy was a good student, so graduation meant that he could go to Georgia Tech, which had a lauded architecture program. Daddy, a very social creature, joined a fraternity and continued his quest to attract his mother's attention. He later told my mother that he never wanted to compete with Ellamae. He had such an artistic side; he could draw and paint and was a fine calligrapher. He could make anything and carve anything, especially from wood. But his world of strong, talented women influenced him to stay out of their realm. At least that's my opinion.

Daddy wrote:

> *"When college came along, I went to Georgia Tech, a state school, because tuition for a state school was $0. Fees were $71.00 for a semester, so my only other expenses were food and board and that was*

very little. I never had enough to pay that on time. I worked at the Sears Roebuck, Buckhead Store. Otherwise, I sold some things I had and I didn't starve, but I never had a penny I didn't already owe somebody.

Things were improving a little the last year before I enlisted, so ever since then, I guess I have been trying to own everything in sight. I never caught up." (notes from Joseph C. League Sr. to his wife, Mary Jane)

Daddy and Jean wrote often, and the affectionate and lengthy letters drew a picture of a sister and brother who had no secrets and sincerely missed one another. Jean had been in Boston for about two years before Daddy left for Tech, so letters meant everything. Talk of their mother was always a part of each letter, writing of her jobs, travel, and social doings. Young Joe frequently begged Jean's tolerance for his shabby stationery and regularly told her of his many endeavors to make money. At one point, he wrote to his sister describing his dating service that was set up to aid his fraternity buddies in finding dates for functions. He boasted that he offered a money-back guarantee but, to date, had had no complaints ending in refunds. Daddy remained creative all of his life.

I cannot find a way to explain the difference in the magical life Jean led in Boston, attending prestigious schools, going to Harvard and MIT dances. Meanwhile, Daddy was working and getting very little financial support, complaining to Jean that his wardrobe was very stretched. But one thing is clear in their letters. Neither was resentful nor questioned it. Neither one ever mentioned that it should be otherwise.

When Joe enlisted in 1941, his letters took on a new tone of seriousness, devotion to the cause, and his interest in flying. This young pilot-to-be clearly had found a passion and loved getting a paycheck. Maybe a passion for something had been the missing ingredient in his life, but the nineteen-year-old, like so many others, was about to become a man.

Jean had many friends who would leave school and enlist just like Joe. The war effort was ramping up and affected everyone in the United States. Food shortages, nylon shortages, and medical shortages all contributed to the feelings of fear and loss that many were suffering, and it was just getting started. It must have been very scary for a young woman to be so far from home and with so many loved ones at risk, but hadn't it been similar for her mother at about the same age?

Ellamae was no stranger to tough times. So, did she come into this world tough as nails or did life form her that way? During her lifetime, horses were replaced by driving machines, and outhouses were replaced with water closets and indoor plumbing. Gaslights and kerosene lamps gave way to electricity, radios brought the news to us faster, movies entertained us, and television entered the living rooms. Planes flew and evolved into jets, satellites orbited the Earth, and men landed on the moon. Atomic and hydrogen bombs were developed, two world wars and the Korean War and the Vietnam War were fought, and nuclear bombs that could destroy whole countries were built – all this in one lifetime. Married at eighteen, just months after the United States entered the action in World War I, Ellamae had moved away from all she'd ever known, with a man who was a mystery. Two of her brothers enlisted and the only contact was letters. Would she ever see them again? In early 1918, the Spanish Flu came on the scene, killing 675,000 Americans and about fifty million in the world. Many of the soldiers were sickened and died. Some states had mandatory orders requiring all people to wear masks. Did these scary times keep Ellamae in Macon with her parents after she fled Shreveport and her new husband? How did George Forrest work his way back into his young bride's life and share a home with her parents for the next four years?

Then came the split, and the really hard times seemed to energize this young woman. In an interview I read, she said educating her children was of foremost importance to her when she found herself alone. Where did that come from? She had four brothers, so did she never feel inferior to men? Why had she left college after only a year to marry?

When I look back at the totality of Ellamae's life and decisions, her marriage is the only line item that doesn't fit her profile. Nothing I can find or conjure makes that line make sense. At this point in her story, I have to let her marriage be the unsolved mystery.

Chapter 7

*"Other people are going to find healing in
your wounds. Your greatest life messages
and your most effective ministry will come
out of your deepest hurts."*

RICK WARREN [23]

There are times in every person's life when the stars align
and circumstances project us into something wonderful or
something terrible. Stir into that our freewill and the
messages taught us by our parents, mentors and history, and
opportunities occur. The entire mix or explosion of events
must then be responded to or acted upon by that individual,
and this is what eventually defines us.

Ellamae was born and grew up in Macon, Georgia.
Today, it is a sleepy little town that has enough
manufacturing and commerce to keep it afloat, but in the
age of Ellamae, it was bustling by any standards. I think it
has value to her story that we look at how her environment

---

[23] Pastor Rick Warren, quilasangles.com

propelled a young woman of bad circumstance to create a place of distinction for herself.

Macon was a railroad hub, and her residents clearly had lofty expectations that their city's central position in the state would always provide for traffic and growth. Many examples of those lofty expectations still exist. The Grand Opera House,[24] built in 1884, was originally known as the Academy of Music. It has one of the largest stages in the country and boasts that BEN-HUR was once performed there with actual chariots on the stage. Many greats were lured to its stage, such as Sarah Bernhardt, Charlie Chaplin, Will Rogers, and even Harry Houdini, to mention a few. In 1936, it became a movie theater.

Saint Joseph's Catholic Church, completed in 1892, remains a glorious and elegant testimony to grand expectations. Though Macon's Catholic community is small, the church is the grandest in town and does not pale next to any basilica or cathedral I have ever visited. The neighborhoods of College Street and old Wesleyan Conservatory, which was the first chartered school for women in the world, suggest that Macon's residents had great faith that Macon was destined to be home to a large population. Not far from Wesleyan, Mercer University grew up, another sign that education and educators were important to the developers of the city. The downtown was a busy and exciting place to be and some fifty or so years from falling into the shadows of Atlanta, her neighbor ninety miles north.

---

[24] See www.thegrandmacon.com

Recently, while visiting the Vintage Macon Georgia website, I learned of an early Macon publication called THE MACON EVENING NEWS that was established in 1884. It gives a glimpse of the growth and grandeur that was in the minds of Macon's builders. The following is an excerpt from the preface of an article posted there about 1891:

"Giving a peep into the past for the purpose of illustrating the present and reflecting the sure brilliancy of the future. It has endeavored to give a picture of the city's material progress and substantial development – a picture of a heaven-flavored city, beautiful and prosperous. It is a picture of her arts and sciences, her churches and colleges, her schools, libraries, elemosynery institutions, her parks, boulevards, public buildings, and her prominent and progressive citizens. Everywhere and in everything, the picture makes Macon attractive. It is attractive in its situation and in its climate, in its location and in its health, in its commercial growth and in its financial soundness, in its religious privileges and in its social opportunities, and in its industrial importance." (Pat Powell's post on Vintage Macon Georgia, September 5, 2020)

******

In the early 1900s, while Ellamae enjoyed her youth and teenage years and sped towards her wedding day, the world was ablaze at the national level and abroad. As far away as the West Coast, Japanese merchants were emerging on the scene but not being welcomed with open arms. In San Francisco and north, the Japanese were treated very cruelly and even driven out. However, their silks and beautiful oriental influence were beginning to be felt all the way to the East Coast.

So many 'firsts' occurred in Ellamae's lifetime that it was hard to keep up with the fast pace. Newspapers were an important business and provided people with a way to learn about one another and the world at large. News was news. People formed their own opinions and shared them on their back and front porches and in their parlors and church halls. A person's worldview came largely from papers, magazines, and neighbors. Newsstand operators 'hawked' the news. My daddy remembers hearing the paperboys shout the headlines even when he was a boy.

Other women around the world were beginning to make their marks. Women in the late nineteenth century were talking about suffrage, equal rights, and discrimination against women. Congress passed an amendment granting women the right to vote after a long, hard fight, on June 4, 1919, and it was ratified on August 18, 1920. One can surmise from Joseph Ellis's letter to young Ellamae's husband that friction in their marriage stemmed from a feeling on Ellamae's part that George Forrest treated her as less than his equal. According to her father and Ellamae, this kind of disregard was not acceptable. This leads me to believe that she and her family perhaps sat around the table often and discussed these issues. Likely, Ellamae was surrounded by brothers who did not suppress her feeling that she could be anything she wanted to be. You have to wonder if George Forrest was looking for a more submissive and traditional wife.

******

Macon, through my dad's eyes, looked something like this:

"We didn't milk cows on College Street but we got milk delivered every day from Solomon Dairy in a big red Dodge truck, driven by the owner, Lint Solomon. The milk was in a glass bottle with a paper stopper and about two inches of cream on the top. They hadn't invented homogenizing yet. The largest bottle was a quart and some people only bought a pint because a quart cost six cents. We didn't have a well in our backyard. The iceman brought ice to the backdoor and put it in the icebox. No problem, because the doors were never locked. We never had a key to a single door in our house. The iceman came in a two-wheeled, mule-drawn wagon and we'd get a nickel or a dime's worth of ice every other day. Deemount, the iceman, cut the large blocks of ice with his pick into smaller ones according to the order, and the smaller pieces were fair game for the kids. The chards were free and the most delicious on a hot summer day.

In the early twenties, if you had a radio, it was only one. They had headsets, so everyone took turns listening and some had one very poor speaker. The radio expert of the house, usually the dad, was constantly turning the only two knobs in an effort to find a sweet spot and less static. Children played games or read when they weren't playing outside.

Toys were homemade, especially during the Depression. Very few people could afford to buy them. Popguns were made from elder limbs and broom handles, rubber guns and swords were made from curtain rods, and skate mobiles were from old worn out remains from a pair of Union Hardware roller skates. Most kids got a pair of skates at Christmas if nothing else. Apple crates or scraps of lumber turned into cars with wheels that came from anywhere you could find them. Mama's clothesline was usually used for steering and clothespins were triggers for rubber guns. Everybody had these because washing machines were still a long way in the future.

Piece goods were the largest section in the department stores because most clothes were homemade. Shoes were of leather, except that boys had high-top Keds. Patterns were available for stylish clothes, but most women made their own, as Ellamae did. Men's clothes were largely store-bought by this time.

Not too far from the College Street apartment in Pleasant Hill, you could find Will Davis's store, partially obscured by a big chinaberry tree and covered in dust from the dirt road that ran past it. There was one very small room in front that was the store and Will and his wife lived in the back. A counter just inside the front door was as far as you could get, and Will would load whatever you wanted right there for you. No paper bags, unless you brought your own. Now this was a spot for a working man or laborer who might have forgotten his lunch or be hankerin' for a few tins of sardines, a chunk of yella cheese, some soda crackers, and a Coke, all for fifteen cents. The six-ounce green glass bottle must be returned for reuse. Then he might amble out and spread his lunch on his lap while sitting on a Coke crate and eat his lunch, knowing full well that his wife would give him hell for forgetting his lunch and wasting fifteen cents, while his whole family could have dined for that. (letter from Joseph C. League Sr. to Bob Tribble, The Wilkinson County News, September 14, 2001)

I am bettin' that my daddy knew enough to tell this story from his own experience at Ira's heels.

Macon's streetcars ran right in front of Ellamae's apartment on College Street, and at the bottom of the hill was an unpaved street called Ocmulgee Street, later Riverside Drive. The car barn was there, so it was a very convenient place to live. It was a nickel to ride and two cents for a transfer.

So it was in early 1929 that Ellamae (twenty-nine) moved up to College Street with Jean (nine) and little Joe (seven). It was a brave move at the dawn of the Depression. A new president, Herbert Hoover, took office and just eight months into his term, the stock market would crash with the country following suit. Hoover could not recover the economy and was a one-term president.

Seven years in her rearview mirror were a marriage and many new chapters added to Ellamae's résumé. Practical application, a year at Fontainebleau, correspondence courses, and mentoring all positioned her for the events that were about to occur.

Knowing her as I did, I feel certain she spent 'no' time dwelling on her choices or her path. A nine-year-old daughter and a seven-year-old son had to be reared and household responsibilities addressed. Besides, there literally was no time for dwelling on feelings. I think it was not in Ellamae's makeup to blame or focus on what was. My evidence would be two children and five grandchildren who never heard her ever mention a husband, a divorce, or an unkind reference to her rough years.

Chapter 8

"Remember to look up at the stars and not down at your feet. Try to make sense of what you see and wonder about what makes the universe exist. Be curious. And however difficult life may seem, there is always something you can do and succeed at. It matters that you don't just give up."

STEPHEN HAWKING [25]

I always felt like I knew my grandmother well. The truth is that I have spent a great deal of time plundering her letters and other people's recollections to tell you what made her tick. My conclusion is that 'love' drove her, and I am surprised at my own findings, but it is the only answer. Then, I had to flounder around to come up with the second part of the equation: who or what did she love that propelled her through her extraordinary life?

Love of her husband doesn't seem a fit. In fact, I think she struggled with this kind of love a great deal, or at least

---

[25] Stephen Hawking Quotes, www.goodreads.com.

her understanding of it. In my father's baby book, I found the following poem that she had cut out of a magazine and tucked in its pages:

WHAT KIND OF WOMAN AM I?

By Marion McLean

Am I the kind of woman who makes fun of her husband before other people?
Or do I consider it no disgrace to be happily married?
Do I know what is going on inside the funny little heads of my children?
Or am I satisfied if they are well dressed, washed, and behave with reasonable mannerliness before guests?
If the living room curtains are clean, do I really care much whether the ice-box is scalded out or not?
Am I strictly honest in making out my household accounts?
Or do I sneak in an occasional shampoo under 'cleaning' and let it go at that?
Which is more important to me – the smocking on the little girl's dresses or the books they read?
Do I take the job of marriage like a good sport, the worse with the better?
Or do I whine for special consideration because, forsooth, I am a woman?
Can I be a good sport and *keep on being one?*
Or after being fine and decent for a while, do I kick over my bucket of milk with a mean dig and then act surprised that no one appreciated the fine quality of milk that I produced?
Do I burn my own smoke?

Or do I discuss my family affairs with my friends?

Would I read a letter that I found in my son's bureau drawer?

Or do I believe that adolescents are people, too?

Do I have my dark gray blankets washed as often as my white ones?

Why don't I?

Can I keep a confidence?

Or do I go tea-potting to my husband with every bit of gossip that turns up?

Do I respect myself and my job, knowing that on the material basis alone a hundred dollars a week would only just replace me in my home?

Or do I sometimes think of myself as a mixture of servant and concubine, with the cringing and rebellion of both?

Am I thin and irritable?

Am I fat and flabby?

Or do I keep fit physically and mentally?

Will my children respect me when I am forty-five?

What will I be like when I am sixty?

What kind of woman am I?

Perhaps this was my most significant finding. Women were in a very different place than we are today. I will remind you that this was tucked in my father's baby book and it was just months after his birth that the final split happened between Ellamae and George Forrest. It might be worth mentioning that there was very little else in the little pale-blue book other than a few recorded gifts and Joe's birth weight of seven pounds and three ounces. Another page lists the date of birth, the doctor's name, the nurse's name, and lastly, the signatures of the parents. Ellamae's name is the only one that appears. When she cut the poem out of the magazine, was it the trigger, and did she realize then and there that she would never fit the mold?

She had given it her all, hadn't she? According to Aunt Ef, Ellamae baked amazing cakes and exceeded at divinity candy and other treats of the day. Did she fit in a home, tending babies and waiting on a man? Was she out of place with small talk and making clothes? Was the company of her brothers and other men more interesting and comfortable to her than that of homemakers and dutiful wives? Had she married a modern man who thought of his wife as his equal? I think not.

A constant in her letters to her children and to her family was their devotion to one another and the kindness they expressed. Ellamae's letters always began with: *"My darlin'"* or some other very affectionate greeting, and their letters to her had the same affections. Literally, hundreds of letters that I have gone through share affection and love between family members and children and are so kind and caring in their tone. Did life just look good on the outside...?

Finding herself divorced and alone to provide for her two children must have felt daunting in 1922. I would imagine that southern ladies were her biggest critics and secretly harbored envy at her bravery but behaved to the contrary. But she didn't look for another man to do it. She did it. In spite of her not being there in so many ways, my dad and his sister vehemently defended her because they never saw her step down or relinquish her duty to them. It was far from perfect, but 'love' drove her to go to work.

Along the way, she loved that she could build things, make them work, and restore order and beauty. Restoration came not in making a marriage work but in making herself work. She never attempted, from what I can tell, to be mother 'and' father. She didn't attempt roles she had no training for, which was probably why her son so frequently said, "She had no idea what to do with me."

Ellamae was terribly real and pragmatic in a fiercely private way, which may sound contradictory because 'real' people are often very transparent. Privacy was a code she lived by, so she didn't make small talk or gossip. She loved purely, giving and expecting absolutely nothing in return. Ellamae had a peace about her that I couldn't understand until I reached my own golden years. The peace came from ashes, like it always does, ashes of loss but with gratitude for all that she had. She never seemed to look back, but she continued to love in a way that required nothing in return. She didn't talk much about love or gush about those she loved, but her actions spoke, and we knew who we were.

I was eleven years old (1956) and in the sixth grade when Ellamae took me to New York. We flew into LaGuardia and back home three days later out of Newark. Mulberry Street Methodist Church was rebuilding, following a devastating fire that had heavily damaged the main sanctuary. Paterson, New Jersey, was home to a leaded stained glass window company that had restored and rebuilt new windows for the church. Ellamae was going there to approve them prior to shipping. It would only take a day, but it was the perfect opportunity to take me and show me New York. We landed just hours after Fidel Castro left following his visit to the U.S. Some who are old enough may remember that he had stayed in Harlem, and the visit was in all the newspapers. We stayed at the Algonquin and ate many of our meals in the famous Rose Room. A car came to take us out to Paterson to see the windows, and Ellamae had the owner give me samples and explain the process to me. I thought it was all about me. I had no idea that she was important or had gone there for anything other than to entertain me. She selected 'Bye, Bye, Birdie' and 'The Miracle Worker' for us to see on Broadway. We took a cab through Central Park and even drove through Harlem to see the banners marking the rooms where Castro had stayed. When we flew home into the Atlanta Airport, it was dark and we still had to drive to Macon. Ellamae never liked to drive, especially at night, and it was raining, making it scary and difficult. Her knuckles were white and I would bet she was scared to death, but she loaded us in, assured me that we would be fine, and struck out onto the dark back roads. I would bet that we were lost for a bit, but she never let on. Climbing that mountain was small potatoes compared to her other obstacles, and she showed no fear that night.

Ellamae

"Jean, darlin', can you hear me? I have so much to tell you about, but I think I am going back to Washington on Wednesday night and I may extend to Boston afterward to see you and Augusta (Aunt Augusta Choate).

"Life is so complicated. Please don't be an architect. I was just home and have to turn around back to D.C. and probably for only a day. There is this most wonderful train called the Southerner and it's so streamlined and made of corrugated metal. No Pullman cars, just all lounge cars. It runs from New Orleans to New York and I'll get on in Atlanta at 8:30 at night and get into Washington by 9:30 the next morning, and the best part of it is that the round trip fare is only $19.00."

"How wonderful, Mother. When did all this happen?" Jean managed to squeeze in.

"I saw the train on exhibition in Washington before it made its maiden voyage and there is a car representing each southern state. Georgia's is peach-colored inside and has photo murals of Stone Mountain and the State Capitol on the walls.

"Oh, Jean, isn't it exciting how easy travel is becoming? Ruth went back to school on it just last week. Of course from Boston, flying is still the best way but the fare is so much more expensive. I checked with the postal telegraph and it's $108.10 round trip. That is a lot of money, but if you want to come home next month for that wedding and you wouldn't get thrown out of school, I'll buy the ticket."

******

'Purpose' is life's elixir. I think people come to their purpose, most often, in midlife after a lot of living has been done. Some never find purpose. It is rare to find when you are self-focused and is sometimes erroneously identified many times before truly being discovered. It is my belief that 'purpose' is necessary before you can have the kind of love and peace that I described Ellamae was possessing. My conclusion is that my grandmother found her purpose many times during her life and deeply settled into her skin in her midlife. She lived beauty and harmony in all of her actions. Just the way she ate a meal – no one was watching, no one knew, but it was with order and design. Courses set out and beautifully presented on China and crystal with silver. All this was simply because it was lovely that way. She dressed simply but with quiet elegance. She loved wools and silks and clothing that felt good and was finely crafted. Her home, and mine, she built with natural redwood that was untreated because she loved the richness of it, and it was combined with old brick that had scars and signs of age. Ellamae loved the stories these natural materials told of growth and struggles. Like life, these old things could be restored and refreshed and reused to build something beautiful. She designed workplaces and homes for others that met their needs and made them beautiful and comfortable as well. In this way, she found a way to support her children and a way to love others and her community by making it beautiful for them. Doing this was what gave her pleasure and the way she could show love.

Even before World War II, Ellamae was setting herself apart from other women in architecture because their work was largely residential. Her practice was not a single-person practice, as had been the norm for women before her; instead, she had brought in two men. She landed numerous commercial jobs as well as residential contracts, and with the emergence of the war, she was positioned to add many more commercial projects. I was impressed to learn that in her first year of practice, she was commissioned to build a service station, a reservoir, two church buildings, six residences, and two restorations. During and after the war, she added several schools and school buildings, many projects for Bibb Manufacturing Company, and many homes, including a Colonial Revival in Sandersville, Georgia, to her works.

Many young architectural novices got their first jobs in Ellamae's office before setting out on their own. It was a busy and exciting workplace. Ellamae's scope included nearly all counties in Georgia and reached as far west as Tucson, Arizona, where she built two private residences. Hospitals and doctor's offices soon came her way, and I particularly remember the stress and largeness placed on her office when she took on the massive addition of the Macon Hospital in the early fifties. Four architects were chosen and she headed up the group. She took on many new people in her office to handle the ever-expanding workload.

My grandmother's office is etched in my mind even to this day. It still exists but, sadly, is hard to connect with the images that I hold so dear. It was a soft beige, one-story, painted brick building nestled between an old turreted building, known by many then as Guy White's and First Presbyterian Church on Mulberry Street. The beautiful old church is moss-covered and looks as though it has been there forever. Across Mulberry Street is the Grand Opera House that I told you about earlier. The street, one of Macon's oldest, is divided by a narrow park that is now named after Ellamae. The many parks in the city had been landscaped and restored by her about 1974, and she always preached their value to keeping downtown viable and inviting. A block up the street is Mulberry Methodist Church, where she was a lifetime member and whose sanctuary and youth center she designed. I feel a special reverence for those beautiful stained-glass windows that I reviewed with her so many years ago. Another block up still stands the Katherine Court Apartments where life on her own first began. It is so fitting that her modern-looking office sits there, dwarfed by structures that came to define Macon and Ellamae herself.

A block in the other direction, toward downtown, is City Hall. When I was a youngster, the Grand Opera House was a movie theater, and my brother and I were sometimes allowed to go to the movies and then cross the street and park back to Ellamae's office to stay with her until she would drive us home with her. Her office was on the front right side of the building, and she could spy us coming from her desk. A huge, solid, heavy glass door opened to a small reception area, and Martha Haynes occupied the desk there. It seemed like a fishbowl from the front, and the door had to be locked and unlocked from the bottom. I can so clearly see my grandmother bend her knees ever so gracefully and bend down by the side of it and put her key in to spring it open with a tug. Perhaps the act of bending to open the door reminded her of her journey to a better life, and the glass, gave a clear view of all that was inside.

On a shopping or movie day when we might go there, the door was open and business in progress. If she were in a meeting or had someone in her office, Martha would intercept us and entertain us herself with beautiful paper and crayons or send us to the drafting area. My brother, Joe Jr., knew he would be an architect from the time he could pronounce it. I really think he was drawing floor plans for houses and buildings when he was seven. He would happily spend hours atop one of the tall drafting-table stools with scales and straight edges, drawing.

It is probably not odd that I should admit that I was in high school before it occurred to me that my grandmother was different from my friends' grandparents. She wasn't at home during the day and didn't have a husband, but as Daddy would have said, "She never did."

She came often to our house and we went often to hers. We never called her anything other than 'Ellamae,' and she clearly was different, but I never noticed. I didn't really know what she did or that it was a man's profession. After all, her daughter was one, too. To add to that, my grandmother on my mother's side was just the opposite. I spent my summers with her and my grandfather on the beach in Margate City, New Jersey. I called them Mom Mom and Pop Pop, and they were lovely and young and clever, but they were also… typical. Mom Mom stayed home, did the cooking herself, made yummy treats, had no secretary, and was right out of a textbook. Still, I was not confused. Looking back, I think I thought geography had a lot to do with it. My winters were spent in the deep south with an architect for a grandmother and my summers were spent on the Yankee beaches of Atlantic City and Margate, with friends and family who were largely Catholic and Jewish as opposed to Southern Baptists and Methodists. I acclimated easily to both and loved being at both places, but it was as different as night and day. Moving from one to the other felt seamless and warm and loving, so I just applied that to my grandmothers.

While Joe was drawing and designing and practicing for his future life, I would be turned loose in the sample room.

There were a few catalogs with pictures, but better yet were tile samples, carpet samples, and fabric samples galore. I had beautiful Madame Alexander dolls that were given to me mostly by Ellamae. I loved to sew and make elegant outfits for them and their fairytale lives that were imagined from my own desires. If the weather was nice and it was not a Sunday, we could play in the courtyard that ran the length of the drafting room. It was grassy and surrounded by a glass wall on one side and a tall brick wall on the opposite side. A small opening was all but hidden to the church side and was designed to keep both courtyards private. We were not allowed to go on the other side of the wall, and for some reason, we were a little afraid to go to the church side. I guess it was just the unknown. Once, or maybe twice, we did disappear behind the wall, but it didn't take long for us to be discovered and punished. Joe and I spent so many wonderful times there. While my brother was at Tech, and before he went into practice in Atlanta, he spent many summers working there like many young men before and after him.

So, you see, Ellamae was a wonderful grandmother and offered us a very unique view.

This brings me right back to her way of loving – often conventional and just as often not. I was Ellamae's regular partner for Macon Little Theater shows after I got to high school. I never remember her belly-roll laughing. Some plays were hilariously funny, but she would never open her mouth that big. Her pale blue eyes would get twinkly and crinkly in the corners, and her lips would draw back and let the quietest laugh escape, but that was it. She never just chatted for no reason. She listened a lot. Paradoxically, in her old letters, she went on and on about who had gone to what with her and what she wore and on and on. I wonder when that left her.

Ellamae practiced a disciplined love or intentional love. Like everything else, it seemed to me that she had a plan, a framework, even for loving. It never seemed random or particularly passionate. That lack of passion probably was misread by most as 'not loving,' but I have come to realize that her affection was very powerful. By 'intentional,' I don't mean that she decided whom she loved but rather that she planned intentionally how to love them. Ellamae accepted you as you were and met you there with her love. She deliberately looked at you as you were and left you there with no feeling that you had disappointed her.

The exception to this might have been my father. I know he never felt like he added up to expectations. Notice that I didn't say 'her expectations.' I think it was in my dad's mind and his own comparisons that left him feeling lacking. He said he never chose architecture because he didn't want to compete with her and his sister. I think it is very likely that Ellamae could see that her son did not fit the mold and needed another path. From my perch, I never saw her push him toward anything. Maybe that alone made him feel that she didn't care. Here is a letter that he wrote to her from Tech:

"Dearest Mother,

Thanks an awful lot for the money. I paid all of my many debts – (personal) and laundry bill, etc. I haven't paid for my meals at the house yet. That's $19.50. I've paid dues and made another payment *on the mid-term dance ticket. We've been paying $1.00 or $1.50 a month on the tickets. I've paid $3.50 so far. The block ticket costs $6.50 for frat men, so I owe $3.00 more. It cost $11.50 for non-frat men.*

I was wrong about Glenn Miller. He's not gonna be here at all. I guess I should have known I was being kidded. Hal Kemp is here now at the Roxy. He is really good, too. Eddie Duchin is gonna play for all of the mid-terms.

Exams are from the 22nd until the 31st. I'm exempt in English, so my exams are from Tuesday through Friday. I'll probably be home right after that and come back up here for the dances.

After paying for debts, dues, and doughnuts (breakfast), I've got about $10 – a little less. I think I owe everybody money. Cigarettes, food, laundry, dues, etc.

If you get a bill from Lew Adler, it's for a wind breaker I bought. They'll probably send me the bill, though.

[He drew a picture of it and labeled it $3.95.]

"It's made of real thin, waterproof, airplane fabric. It won't wrinkle. It can be worn as a shirt or jacket and the wind can't get through it. It's soft material, beige-colored, and I've used it for a raincoat, jacket, and a shirt.

I won't have much time to be going anywhere, but I'll try to go by and see Uncle Herbert.

I've been going to the neighborhood skating rink in my spare time. I think it'll make my ankle stronger. Everybody there is a wonderful skater. I wonder if it would be possible to send my skates up. I've got some real expensive rink skates that I got from Herbert Mabry. Clara probably knows where they are.

I got your letter late on Sunday night. The delivery service stinks. I'll explain exactly where all the money went when I see you. Believe it or not, it wasn't on foolishness – not a bit of it.

This letter is in pencil because I'm outta ink.

Lotsa love,
Joe (Letter from Joe League to Ellamae League)

******

She had a steel frame with a soft belly. She never slumped even in her nineties, displaying her steel. When she did suffer or was sick, she dug in quietly and did what she needed to do. At sixty-seven or sixty-eight, Ellamae broke her collarbone but was insistent that she could manage alone. She described to me that she could sit up without help by bending her knee up and grabbing it with her good hand. She would then slowly straighten her knee which would move her to a seated position. That was the engineer in her blood. The soft middle was her selflessness and her complete and total giving with absolutely 'no' expectations.

Ellamae had a mild stroke in her early seventies, which likely led to the final closing of her office. Initially, her speech was affected, and the way she described it was that she knew what she wanted to say, but it didn't come out the way she intended. Few people even knew about it, and she would not receive guests until she was confident that her speech issues had resolved. I was never afraid for her because she never let us know to worry.

At some point, likely after her stroke, we became aware that she felt uncomfortable on her steps, so she was bumping down on her bottom to ensure her safety. You'll recall that her house was a split-level, and her bedroom and the only bath were on the second floor. She lived alone, and the landing of her stairs was home to the only telephone in the house. The steps were completely open on one side with no rail on either side. Daddy and Jean argued to no avail that a second phone needed to be installed by her bed and that the steps needed a rail. That was another battle she won. After closing her office, Ellamae did set up a desk in her living room and allowed another phone there.

******

Christmas was magical at our house. We weren't wealthy, but Christmas was the one time of year that it felt like we were. Big gifts did not happen for most kids except at Christmas in those days. We'd wait all year for a special something that we were longing for. My New Jersey grandparents sent money to each of us, and that was a big treat because it was the only time we had money of our own. Ellamae came to our house on Christmas Eve, and she came late. Joe and I would go to bed late and be slow to settle after leaving snacks for Santa. Only when we were asleep would she bring her gifts for us from her car and put them under our tree. It was easy to spot hers because they would be so beautifully and perfectly wrapped. Joe Jr. never made it much past 4:30 a.m., but we had to promise not to go in before daylight and not to open any wrapped packages before our parents joined in. Ellamae never was there for the opening of what were always our most desired things. She never wanted credit or a fuss, but she did come for steak-and-egg breakfast, despite the fact that we would all have Christmas dinner at her house just a few hours later.

"Come give your granny a hug," were words that never left her lips. There was no large bosom to nestle into and no baby talk that you might imagine from a grandmother. My friends didn't know what to make of her and sometimes were uncomfortable with this woman. Some found themselves reviewing their manners and searching for Emily Post's tips.

I can recall how Ellamae shied away from fuss and notoriety and never participated in a conversation complimentary of her. It truly aggravated her to be asked about being a 'woman' architect. I could see her color rise at the distinction. About the time I went to Wesleyan, the women's lib movement was brimming in the world, and women reporters and young budding females in architectural school could not wait to have her join their cause and speak out. What was missing for Ellamae, though, was the thought that this was new or the idea that it needed a movement. Whatever the odds, a woman could clearly forge her own path, and hadn't she? She was particularly put off by women who tried to look like men and dress in pants in the workplace. Remember, Ellamae was quite formal, and she always wore skirts or dresses at the office. Not until she retired and closed her office in 1975 did she take to wearing slacks.

In a 'Macon Telegraph & News' article written after she was awarded the Bernard B. Rothschild Award, the author was spanked for trying to suggest womanhood was important.

> *"A petite woman with intense features, Mrs. League started in the profession in 1922, a time when women as architects were a rarity. She doesn't like to dwell on that fact.*
> *"'I was always an architect, not a woman architect but an architect. I encourage women going into the profession not to concentrate on being separate as a woman but to concentrate on being a good architect.'"* (*Macon Telegraph & News*, 1975: ID)

The Atlanta Constitution published an article entitled "Fifty-three Years in Architecture, But She Was No Maverick, " [26]written by Helen C. Smith and published just a few months after Ellamae closed her office in October of 1975. She reacted with surprise when the reporter used the term 'maverick' and remarked that if she was one, she didn't know it. The seasoned architect described herself as

---

[26] "53 Years in Architecture, But She Was No Maverick," *Atlanta Constitution (December 18,1975:34.)*

'a woman who was doing what she was most interested in to support her family.'

"Architecture has to follow the trends in living. There are new materials, new technologies, new lifestyles, and no craftsmen who are able to copy tradition." This is another of her quotes that reminds me of her approach to life in general. Life's moving tides must be embraced and adaption made if one is to be successful.

It is doubtful if Ellamae ever lost sleep wondering if she had won someone's love, much as I might, for instance. She just loved them and requested no dividends. She was quite rare in that respect. I don't think she started out that way, but my guess is that someone who needed her or depended on her would have felt like a very heavy burden. She was happiest when others expected nothing, and it freed her to give and give and give. Her currency was her ability to design a better place for you to live, be it mental or physical.

As best I can recall, Ellamae took Joe Jr. and me to Miami to see her parents in 1949 or 1950. Grand Susie and Grand Joe, to us, were getting on in years and had never met us. Likely, traveling was out of the question for them, so Ellamae put us, then five and six, aboard our first Eastern Airlines flight for a daytrip to Miami with her. It was such an adventure, and Mother had us decked out in our Sunday best.

I can remember a small one-story house with a screen door to the backyard that was fenced in. I can remember a heavy pitcher with a block of clear ice and full of lemonade and sandwiches that were served in the backyard. Had I been older, I would have snooped around and wanted to see the room my father slept in as a boy, and I would have fished for some stories about my dad, his sister, and my grandmother. My memory of my great-grandparents is only that they seemed very old and looked nothing like my grandmother. Grand Joe died in January of 1954 at eighty-three and Grand Susie in 1955 at eighty-one. Joe and I understood our grandmother's purpose that day, so we played and chatted to let them know us. It was a short afternoon because we soon took a cab back to the airport and back to Macon, having helped Ellamae love her parents.

Chapter 9

"Life is amazing. And then it's awful. And then it is amazing again. And in between the amazing and the awful, it's ordinary and mundane and routine. Breathe in the amazing, hold on through the awful, and relax and exhale during the ordinary. That's just living heartbreaking, soul healing, amazing, awful, ordinary life. And it's heartbreakingly beautiful."

L.R. KNOST [27]

And so it was for Ellamae – ups and downs and highs and lows. Like all of us, what defines us is how we learn from the blows.

Some of us are just gifted with resilience, or what we call 'grit.' Some are taught by life or those around us to pick ourselves up, dust ourselves off, and start all over again. Those are a song's lyrics, I am certain. I can even remember the tune but not the composer. It is a theme of life with which we are all familiar as we go along our own roads. Our faith and longing to give more to those behind us than we

---

[27] L.R. Knost, *Two Thousand Kisses A Day: Gentle Parenting Through The Ages and Stages*, www.goodreads.com.

ourselves had is within us in an unexplainable way. It seems to me that it just is there, like an indwelling yearning much like faith and our deep desire for God. The difference is that we don't all have that faith or need for God, but I have yet to know of a civilization or a person who does not wish to leave our world better than we found it for those who come behind us, a blind force within us.

For her years as a parent, a single parent, I don't think many guidelines were written. Today, guidance is more common, and every magazine has advice for divorced women and single parents. Every movie and novel cover these stories endlessly, but Ellamae had to forge her own way and seemed to spend as little time as possible thinking about it or apologizing to anyone about it.

Young Joe was a handful of mischief and with interests very different from his mother's. Ira was nearby to temper his wildness and teach him right and wrong and good from evil. Joe constantly remarked that his mother had no clue about what to do with him, but never did he mention or complain that he didn't have a father. Never did he speak of longing to know about his dad or about daydreaming about a father.

I imagine that few of his friends shared the same kind of story as him, but I do know that many of his friends were fatherless, perhaps from World War I or because people just died younger in those years from illnesses, heart attacks, strokes, and so forth. Women died in childbirth much more frequently in those days, and flu and tuberculosis were killers. Young Joe and Jean were by no means alone or odd on that front. Certainly, that accounts for some of their lack of curiosity about their father.

Jean, on the other hand, was the oldest and a lovely young lady who followed the norms of the times, sharing many interests with her fashionable, elegant mother. I have many letters between Jean and Ellamae while Jean was in Boston in school – boarding school, then Radcliffe, Smith and Harvard. The letters are full of excitement about grades, boyfriends, friends, dresses, and invitations. The greetings and closings of each letter spilled over with love and affection between them, and I sometimes feel like I am reading a fairytale. After Jean graduated and returned home to Macon to join her mother's practice, I was born and Daddy (Joe) moved us to Macon. My earliest memories are magical when it comes to my grandmother and my Aunt Jean. I watched them dress for dates and saw flowers delivered to their house and beautiful dresses laid out on the beds. Ellamae's very modern office was full of fancy people who fussed over Joe Jr. and me, and the world felt like 'love' was all around to a little girl like me.

The post-World War II years I was born into were giddy for a while for most. For just as many, sadly, life would never be the same. Men and women came back without limbs, crippled, sick at heart, or in body bags. Most were in need of civilian jobs and housing for themselves and often families whom they were just meeting. Though hard in many ways, a feeling of hope and a sense of oneness filled hearts and replaced the fear and horror of the years of war. A brief lull existed.

Letters! I think it so important to discuss letters and how they were in those days. It was over half a century before laptops and emails and Facebook would arrive on the scene, replacing the handwritten notes and stationery that revealed so much about the people who were writing. At the turn of the century, the very paper used spoke volumes about the station of the writer. Following World War I, life became a little simpler and less formal, but people literally chronicled their lives to their parents, lovers, wives, husbands, aunts, uncles, and friends. One thing that strikes me as I read so many of these characters' letters is how personally and privately they spoke to one another. The letters are intended for the addressee 'only.' They reveal a great deal of passion and love that they rarely spoke in person but would say in something akin to poetry in their letters. The love and affection of the greetings is so intimate and designed for that person alone. They vary from child to child or show great respect and affection for parents and family members. The exchanges are very positive and gratuitous and uplifting for the most part. The other thing I noticed is how informational they are. I feel I really know the people who wrote these hundreds of letters that I pored through and can glimpse their world and their relationships. Sadly, it is a lost art.

Here is one that I especially like from Jean to her brother, Joe, about 1939. You can feel her big sisterliness.

Thursday

Dearest Joe,

It snowed today, doggone it! Nice and deep, too. Makes me mad 'cause we'd actually had a few days with sunshine and no snow. I even wrote Mother to send my spring stuff. Tell her for me that she can even send those summer dresses if she wants to. I won't really need them till the end of April, though.

Thanks for the clipping of Sue – that's a darn good picture of her, don'tcha think? I haven't written her yet but I'm goin' to.

That would be wonderful if you all could get Bunny Berrigan for the dances. He played at Woodberry last year – the time I didn't go.

How's your saxophone? You promised to learn to play it before I get home. Remember?

I went to a lecture today on the art of Walt Disney. They have a lot of original drawings at the Fogg Museum and Mr. Field used slides from the drawings in his lecture. Mr. Field is really wonderful. He teaches a crazy course in abstract design that I wanted to take next year and now he's getting kicked out. He's too radical for the blue bloods of 'Hahvahd.'

Ruth's going home on March 22nd, so you'll see her soon. How's Agnes these days? Neither Ruth nor I have heard from Rudolph since we went to Vassar. Don't know what we did wrong.

Saturday

It's snowing again. It might as well be January. Snookie and Stacy and I went in town for lunch today at the Russian Bear. They took me to lunch on account of my checkbook is having a spell and I didn't think it should be disturbed. We even had champagne cocktails. That's where I wanted to take you and Mother when you were here. We couldn't have taken Aunt Choate, though, so I didn't visit.

I went out with Drip last night, like a dope. We had a right good time 'cause he's not a bad dancer. We went to Steuban's, where I went with Peter once, and they had a good floor show, so I didn't have to look at him much. The payoff was when he walked in looking like Joe College in a raccoon coat! They are so ridiculous-looking.

I wish I knew what you wanted for your birthday. I hate to give you stationery again, though you could probably use it.

With sisterly affection,

Jean (letter from Jean League to brother, Joe)

From 1937 until 1945, Jean and Daddy wrote often and only saw each other for short visits. Many of these letters, like this one, were written over several days. They were started, added to, and then, finally sent. They told stories and contained feelings that gave you a real sense of who the writer was. They were so conversational. College and then the war kept the family apart, but their closeness remained intact because of their letters.

In 1950, I was five and we had not long before moved into our house on Waverland Drive, just up the street from Ellamae. It is still there and was built out of redwood, just like hers. Ours is a one-story ranch that earned a spot on the National Register of Historic Places because it was unique in its purpose. Daddy's sister, Jean, designed it, and it was so distinctive that it was published in several magazines. The magazine I remember most vividly was called

'Progressive Architecture,' and the construction dust was barely swept away when the photographer, Richard Garrison, arrived in his Packard to spend the day with us and take the photos for the article.[28] I can be seen in two of the photos, one of which is with my dog, Butch. The photographer's shiny car was propped in the carport to give it a more 'lived-in' look. The article itself bears mentioning here because it describes the new kind of housing needed for so many young couples like my parents and how their needs had changed following the war. Here are a few paragraphs from that article that I promise you would not find in a magazine today:

To Georgia farmers,

The ubiquitous plantation field shed with its tin roof white in a summer sun and its thin stilts supporting sharply angled planes has a humble familiarity. To the critic or designer, it is a humility nearing eloquence. Set deep among longleaf pines, this suburban Macon house faces west, on a site sloping to the south.

It was planned for a budgeting, servant-less couple with two children, who sought utility and privacy. They wanted a design suitable to the area – one devoid of pretense and display. To do this, the architects closed the street side of the house and grouped rooms around an interior terrace. Materials and colors were chosen as a relief from the faded red brick of neighborhood homes. Redwood siding contrasts with oyster-white asbestos shingles, recalling the infinity of shining roofs

---

[28] *Progressive Architecture* (July 1953): 102-104.

atop gnarled-plank farm sheds. Within its limitations of convention, there seem to follow a solution consistently sympathetic.

That last sentence really caught my attention. It not only describes the house I grew up in and the house my parents shared for sixty-three years but it aptly describes my grandmother. 'Within its limitations of convention…' could be within 'her' limitations… 'There seems to follow a solution consistently sympathetic.' She solved things 'consistently sympathetic' to the land, the needs, and the desires of the client. She could thrill clients by restoring or designing spaces in her non-traditional way in her way of loving.

The homily delivered at Ellamae's funeral by Rev. Vance B. Mathis made it obvious to me that though few knew her mysteries, some could see deeply and see what I saw. He was making the point that architects and theologians deal with the seen and unseen, not just what is visible is known. He said:

"Life is like that. We're all in the architectural and construction business. These bodies are merely the scaffolding, obscuring our inner selves, where the real work of building the spiritual life is going on. We're constructing buildings for eternity. And as Ellamae League was making our world grander with physical buildings, she was at the same time erecting a grand spiritual building within. She was a person of strength who had learned through rigorous experience the need for a healthy balance between independence, self-assurance, and courage and the qualities of dependence, self-surrender, and openness for guidance. Her faith meant something to her, as did her church." (Homily at the funeral of Ellamae Ellis League by Vance B. Mathis, March 8, 1991)

Now there is a word that really fits: 'self-surrender.' It is a very unusual quality and one that I believe defines her as well as any. More than anyone I have ever known, my grandmother looked life in the face and worked with whatever was in front of her.

She loved things and people that were real – things made of real materials that felt old and true. She loved to take old things and rework them to retain their beauty but polish them up in a restored way that spoke of a past. She was quoted as saying, "I love downtown. I wouldn't be caught dead at a mall."

Old downtown with the memories and the stories were where it was at for Ellamae. It could be new or added to, but it needed to be nestled into the arms of the old. Maybe it was just saving old trees or carefully crafted views, but leveling all that was before and ignoring the history was not her game.

Old buildings and their pasts did not scare her. It may seem contradictory that she designed many contemporary buildings, like her own office and the Scottish Rite Temple and many residences to name just a few. These were structures that were born new from nothing and they

required new vision and a forward look. Not contradictory
at all, really!

Chapter 10

"Write it on your heart that every day is the best day in the year. He is rich who owns the day, and no one owns the day who allows it to be invaded with fret and anxiety. Finish every day and be done with it. You have done what you could. Some blunders and absurdities no doubt crept in. Forget them as soon as you can. Tomorrow is a new day; begin it well and serenely, with too high a spirit to be cumbered with your old nonsense. This new day is too dear, with its hopes and invitations, to waste a moment on the yesterdays."

RALPH WALDO EMERSON[29]

1942

Joe League

"I have written you all about how flight school is going, and this call is costing me a pretty penny, so tell me where we

---

[29] Ralph Waldo Emerson, *300 Good Morning Quotes & Images*, https://wisdomquotes.com.

are on the ring. I know it is gonna be pricey, but I will send you another payment this week."

"Slow down, Joe. Call me back collect. There's too much to tell." Ellamae hears the call disconnect, and in moments, the operator is back on the line.

"Mr. Orr called me in today to look at another star sapphire, but I think the other one, the first one is really prettier. I just don't wanna pick it on my own, sugar. Tell me what you want me to do…"

"Wish I could get home, but no way. A couple of guys here have already wiped out, and that ain't gonna happen to me. Just go with the first one, Mother. I definitely want platinum. Three diamonds on each side just like the picture I drew."

"Okay, Joe. That's done. Now, I have to tell you about Mary Jane's visit. We all really hated that you couldn't make it, but Jean did a great job introducing her to all your friends. I sho' do wish Jean was here so she could tell you all about it."

"You are killin' me, Mother. Tell me. She's gorgeous, isn't she? Start at the beginning."

"Jean met her train. We figured she'd be exhausted from the travel, so we didn't have much planned that day. Jean said she felt so school-girlish in a cotton shirtwaist 'cause MJ stepped off the train, fresh as a daisy, in a little green suit with gloves and pumps. Jean thought she was so elegant. She knew from her pictures that it was her. Think they hit it off right from the start.

"We had supper here and just let her catch her breath. She's easy to be with but I don't think she packed well for our heat. Next morning, we took her to the office and Ollie and Delmar just ate her up. They were real happy that she doesn't sound too Yankee. They think she'll fit right in, but I hope we didn't overwhelm her. Anyhow… we took her to the club that night and stayed out real late. Jean and her friends all took her out the next night and she looked real nice and was all dressed up. I went home after supper and left them to dance the night away. They're not too many of your friends here 'cause the war has called all you able-bodied boys.

"Joe, I like her a lot. I really do. She seems just fine and handles herself really well. I think Jean just loved her. 'But,' I think you need to wait until all this is over because I just don't know how you are goin' to make it on your pay. If you make grade and stay in, then get married. She'll wait."

"Mother, I am gonna make grade and I am gonna fly. I think I'll settle in and be happier if we go ahead. We've talked and she's willing and we're both saving every dime. Soon as I'm commissioned and get my wings, I'll be making better money. Most guys are already married.

"Can you believe this is me? Finally settled in to one girl?"

"Well… this call is gonna cost me big bucks, but I'll get the ring all finished up. It's goin' to be beautiful. Just think you need to wait on those wings."

So, after a long ride on a troop train with her mother in tow, Mary Jane Proebstle married Joseph Choate League in Waco, Texas, on September 29, 1943. He got his wings, commissioned, and married in the same week. Eleven years later, Jean married Charles E. Newton III in Macon. The war would end in 1945, and so much would change. In 1944, Ellamae was admitted to the American Institute of

Architects. In 1952, commercial flights would emerge on the scene, and this opened the world to so many. Ellamae found herself breaking traditions in many ways as she established Macon's chapter of AIA. Meanwhile, the same year she was elected as president of the Georgia chapter of the AIA, and in 1963, she was installed as the first president of the Georgia Council of Architects, (now the Georgia Association of Architects).

There was never a time that I noticed her slowing down or was aware that she was so busy. Her office was an exciting environment and almost always had students and apprentices eager to get a gig there. Ellamae loved teaching and having new blood around. I imagine that it was stimulating and also afforded her the opportunity to stay current. She was at her finest among her peers, and she traveled constantly to Atlanta because of her involvement in the Georgia American Institute of Architects. Jordon Jelks, who worked for her for many years, said that she kept the office small and always filled with young apprentices, each of whom had their own voice and influence. In her office, they could learn how to bring a project to fruition, something they couldn't get in school.

Money was never a driver and, certainly, Ellamae wasn't interested in acquiring 'things.' She made her surroundings pleasing and enjoyed travel and gift-giving but was actually very content with just what she needed and not much excess. She was not interested in air-conditioning, television, fancy stoves, or dishwashers. She loved to read and go to plays, to entertain, and to be quiet. I think Ellamae's down time was as important to her as her busy time. I would seriously doubt that she was ever bored, and it seemed to me she did everything very deliberately. For instance, she packed for travel several days in advance and with a plan. Large sheets of tissue were placed between the layers of her clothing and the folding was so precise as to allow for no wrinkles or folds. Shoes were individually wrapped and placed so that they surrounded the outside of the luggage to add support. The choices for the trip were arranged in order so that she would have to disturb things as little as possible. Her jewelry was always simple and artistic and often colorful. She loved Mexican silver and turquoise was a favorite color of hers. She never wore a watch, but in her later years, Ellamae regularly wore a gold initial ring. How tragic it would have been to rifle through her things at an airport, as she might be subject to today!

******

April 6, 1970

Opening Night of the Restored Grand Opera House

"Thank you, Joe, for driving me. I hate to make you do this, but the limo is taking more than just me," Ellamae explains.

"Mother, you look amazing. Don't worry. I love doing it and you hate to drive at night. Besides, Mary Jane loved getting to see you ahead of time because we'll probably not be able to see you at the red carpet."

"A limo is really not necessary."

"You deserve every minute of it, and I just want you to enjoy yourself. We're right on time with a few minutes to spare. I'll walk you in."

"Joe, afterwards find me, can you? The steps and the reception… I'll be fine but the steps make me nervous."

Just a few weeks earlier, a letter had come with all the last-minute instructions for the opening of the Grand Opera House. It was the end of a huge amount of labor and love. The grand old building had stood there longer than Ellamae had lived, and it was the view from her office window since 1940. Her first office had been inside the grand building on the third floor. She and the old building had many years together. It would have been a cryin' shame had the old landmark been destroyed, and it was her doing, along with so many on the council, to save it. Now it was as glorious as the day it was built, and it was restored to grandeur, with all its stories safe in its walls. Just the next block up was Mulberry Street Methodist Church and Ellamae knew its treasures, too. Both old buildings grew up with her; they were going to have some more years together, and both were full of her fingerprints. Ellamae had truly loved each and every project because they reflected what she did best. She found life and beauty in building things and bringing comfort to all who saw them and went inside. These two projects were more. They were her heart and soul. They held her own history in so many ways, but more than that, they served Macon, the only home she'd ever known.

I think it's fair to say that Ellamae did 'not' excel at motherhood. Babies never seemed to be her forte, but as her own children grew older, she settled in comfortably to being with them. I would go so far as to say that her skills greatly improved with 'their' age.

There were other things she didn't do well, like being a wife. She accepted her weaknesses and did the best she could out of love. She looked about herself and found her strengths – her gifts – and discerned her calling.

Many live life with the ending of their story in mind. Some start out wanting to hold a particular office or do a particular thing to contribute to society or make a contribution so their name lands in the history books. Ellamae's was not such a story. She let her life events take her where she was going in the large part. I think that she liked her story in the end and was well satisfied, but I think that she did not want it to include many of the things I have written about here. My intention is not to tarnish her because I still love the ending.

Sometimes my heart hurts for Jean and Daddy because they got the least of her, but for the rest of us, she was magnificent.

******

March 4, 1991

"We've been here for hours, Jean, but I don't think we should leave. Are you okay to stay? You need to call anyone?"

"No, Joe. Let's just sit close by so she knows we're here. She looks so small and frail."

Ellamae

"I can hear you, you know.

Good bye, my loves… All is well with me."

Afterword

"Be the person who breaks the cycle. If you were judged, choose understanding. If you were rejected, choose acceptance. If you were shamed, choose compassion. Be the person you needed when you were hurting, not the person who hurt you. Vow to be better than what broke you – to heal instead of becoming bitter so you can act from your heart, not your pain."

LORI DESCHENE[30]

In the beginning, I told you that this book would not be about Ellamae League's architectural achievements because these have been documented again and again. I promised you stories that would help you to know Ellamae on a more personal level, one that might add a new dimension to her amazing life.

Just a month after my father died, in February 2016, Wesleyan College invited me to be a special guest at the

---

[30] Lori Deschene, *Tiny Buddha, Simple Wisdom for Complex Lives*, https://tinybuddha.com.

award presentation for three Georgia Women of Achievement, one of whom was Ellamae. No other family members were able to attend that morning, so I drove down to Macon by myself, and a dear friend who lives in Macon went with me for support. I was still reeling from my dad's death and the move that followed, and though the idea of writing this book had been on my mind for years, the day solidified my desire.

The other two women being honored had amazing contributions and had many family members present. A film had been produced about each woman, and the families had participated in a big way in all but the one of my grandmother. Daddy was ill, my cousins and brother were involved in other very legitimate things, and I was overwhelmed assisting my dad through his last days. The other two films were wonderful, and I felt like I glimpsed their lives and achievements in a way that I would always remember. Historians had put together the film of my grandmother, and it included every award she'd ever received, many pictures of her, and the works she had designed. In fairness, it was the best they could do without some inside help, but I wanted to cry and called my brother, sister, and my two cousins to commiserate. I felt an overwhelming need to tell the world that she was so much more and had her own stories worth telling that might interest others. They might make her more memorable than just her designs.

I do, however, think that it is important to list the many awards and memberships she had somewhere in this book so the total story exists here. Here they are:

1. Lifetime member of Mulberry Methodist Church
2. Member of the Board of Macon Little Theater for Forty Years
3. Served as President of Business & Professional Women's Club
4. Served with both the Georgia Department of Mental Health Citizens' Council and the Bibb County Board of Health
5. Member of the American Institute of Architects (AIA)
6. First President of the Georgia Chapter of AIA
7. Chairman of Atlanta Chapter Committee of Student Affairs
8. Received National Association of Student Affairs Award
9. Alumnae Award for Distinguished Achievement from Wesleyan College
10. Ivan Allen Sr. Award for Community Service
11. Bronze Medal from Georgia AIA
12. First architectural recipient of the Bernard B. Rothschild Award
13. Awarded Fellowship in AIA, the first and only woman in FAIA
14. Georgia Women of Achievement Award, posthumously
15. Collection of E. E. League Architectural Drawings housed in Genealogy & Historical Room at Washington Memorial Library in Macon

This is certainly an impressive list and well worth mentioning. I hope I have brought her to life in such a way that she feels real, scared, vulnerable, and extraordinary. She was a woman who repurposed herself in so many ways.

I am deeply grateful for the part of her that courses through my veins and the beautiful things she added to my life and most especially for the stories and memories.

Like any book, I have so many people to thank, but sadly, many are no longer on this Earth. Daddy's and Jean's letters have provided so many of the dates and events that are in these pages. My brother, Joe Jr., who sadly I lost a few years ago saw most of these events from his perch just fifteen months higher than mine. He was her future, much as Jean had been, because he learned at her heels and taught her what was new. Architects all.

As for all the help from the living, there were so many. My two first cousins, Jean's daughters, Suzy Newton and Edith Newton Wilson, have filled in so many blanks and offered up research and photos during this process. I didn't have to beg for their stories because they were so willing to share and always ready with dates, photos, and love.

I need to give special thanks to a Macon friend, Carol Clark Robeson, who egged me on from the beginning and accompanied me that day to Wesleyan. Her neighbor at that time was Rick Hutto, who is an author himself. She insisted that we meet and set it all up. He knew my father well and knows a great deal about Macon. The day after we met, my email blew up with information that he had gotten that really pushed me into action. Again, when I had actually finished the book, Rick came to my rescue by helping me through the next steps, and I will forever be indebted. This is a first for me, and Rick was good enough to take me by the hand and he walked me to Mary Pearson, a copyeditor, with whom I enjoyed collaborating. Many thanks to Rick and Mary for their contributions.

I had gotten off to a great start and seemed to be turning my dream into reality when my brother got sick and stole my heart and mind for nearly a year until he died in 2018. He and I sat for hours reliving many of the things I have written about here. In the course of his journey, I was diagnosed with breast cancer and chose to have a double mastectomy as my treatment. I really believed that during my convalescence, I would have ample time to get back to writing and finish my book. Quite the contrary happened. Joe's downturn, added to my own recovery, left me just short of brain-dead, emotionally speaking. I put the book down for the better part of that year.

My excuses not to get back to it ran out, and I began in earnest to research and write again. Many of the letters I had read so long ago needed re-reading, so I did it. I still had piles and piles to go through and pictures galore. It was easy to get lost in the letters, and originally, I wanted to do a compilation, but instead I decided to try and bring Ellamae to life in my own words.

My brother's only child, Elisabeth League Irwin, has been involved in writing herself. Just out of college, she worked for Lynne Cheney while she was the 'second lady' and writing children's books. Elisabeth also helped her father-in-law, who has authored at least two books. She helped me by reading this while it was in formation.

My dear college friend Martha Pafford Schindhelm has steered me and given me so much encouragement after reading this along the way as it took shape.

In ways they will never understand, my three daughters, Mary Clare Dennis Ewing, Catherine Dennis Fruechtenicht, and Caroline Dennis Campbell, who between them produced eight beautiful and genius grandchildren, gave me the purpose and desire to tell this story.

My husband, Don Dennis, is a doctor and has been innovative and smart and contributed so much to so many through his generosity and medical contributions. Twice in our married life, people asked me what it was like to be married to a genius. What am I, chopped liver? Seriously, I decided I wanted to leave something on this Earth that might inspire others and would provide as complete a story as I could conjure to those of us who are a part of this unique person. On one hand, I wish my father had written this book because he was a master storyteller. On the other hand, I am grateful he left it to me because the research has delighted and entertained me for nearly four years.

Both of my parents and my mother's father were voracious readers, and I inherited the gene. The more I read, the more I wanted to write, so this is my second attempt. In 2015, my mother died at ninety-one, and my sister and I were with her at the end because my father, who was ninety-three at the time, could not bear to see her die. They were married for seventy-two years and he was of a very sound mind, but it was a gift that he could not give her. At first, I was angry that he scurried away each day from her hospice room, pretending that there was no need to say goodbye, but after seventy-eight days (an in-hospice record), she was ready and slipped away. That night, after my drive home from Macon to Atlanta, I saw angels three times, and it was a story that I had to tell and leave for my children and grandchildren. Yes, you read that right, 'angels' – Seven huge ones that appeared to me three times. Now I am grateful that Daddy let me have that gift by leaving me no choice but to be at her side. I self-published a little book of the story and it flowed from me with such ease that I hardly felt it came from me. It gave me confidence to tell you this story, and though this one required much more investigation and research than I had ever imagined, it was, again, effortless.

There is a part of writing this book that has been difficult, and that is the 'spirit of Ellamae' who gives me a strong slap now and then. I am certain she would hate this book and hate that I have uncovered so many things that she would have liked buried. She would see no need at all for me to drudge up the personal parts of her life that she found no need to revisit. So, why have I? The truth is that I find her even more worthy of admiration, and I am more awestruck than I already was knowing that she had warts. I started the story because I wanted people to know that she was a tough young girl who took an unusual route to accomplish more than anyone might have thought. I hoped her spirit would inspire others who might feel resigned to a fate. In her case, even her quietness was her strength, but she needed someone else to tell her story. Along the way, the letters I found opened door after door that helped explain her. Seeing clearly fills in so many blanks, and her accomplishments seem more attainable for others because she was as real as the next girl who made mistakes. Pray that I don't enter the pearly gates to find her waiting for me to explain myself.